Guidelines in Art

Murphy & Murphy

Hutchinson

London Melbourne Sydney Auckland Johannesburg

Hutchinson Education Ltd.

An imprint of Century Hutchinson Ltd.
62-65 Chandos Place, London

Century Hutchinson Publishing Group (Australia) Pty Ltd.
16-22 Church Street, Hawthorn, Melbourne, Victoria 3122

Century Hutchinson Group (NZ) Ltd.
32-34 View Road, PO Box 40-086, Glenfield, Auckland 10

Century Hutchinson Group (SA) (Pty) Ltd.
PO Box 337, Bergvlei 2012, South Africa

First published by Folens Publishing Company Limited 1985

© Folens Publishing Company Limited 1985

This edition 1986

Printed at the press of Folens Publishing Company Ltd.

ISBN 0 09 165421 1

Acknowledgements

The authors and publishers would like to thank the following for graphics supplied for use in this textbook:

The Derek Hill Collection for *Westown, Tory Island*; The Bridgeman Art Library for *The Carpenter's Household/ L'Absinthe / Frustuck im Auteuer / Cornfield & Cypress Trees*; Picturepoint Ltd. for *Une Baignade*; The Victoria and Albert Museum for *Lionesses*; Impact Posters for *Oxo Poster*; The Royal Hibernian Academy of Arts for *Day Interior-Exterior/ Tuscany / Moore Street Market / In the Greenhouse / Girl Sewing*; The Ulster Museum for *Dawn, Killarey Bay*; The National Gallery for *Convent Garden, Brittany*; Anne Siggins for *The Melvyn Tuttle Trio*; Michael Grogan, R.T.E. Design Department for *Set Designer*; Dún Laoighre School of Art & Design for screenprinting visuals.

A special word of thanks to *SLIDE FILE* **for slides provided and for their general photographic assistance with this text.**

Table of Contents

1 Visual Awareness

Visual Awareness is a state of mind found in a person who is keenly interested in the visual world; such a person is observant, with a well developed curiosity for colour, shape and texture. Day to day objects are not quickly passed over and taken for granted, because it is from the world around him that the interested observer derives most of the information which stimulates his imagination to create new ideas.

This state of mind is not peculiar to those who are painters; others with keen visual awareness are architects, potters, actors, mime artists, fashion designers, etc. All these people learn from what they see, and use the information thus accumulated to develop their art.

— Work where a keen sense of visual awareness is essential —

Fig. 1.1 (a)   T.V. Programme Set Designer

Fig. 1.2 (b)   Carpet Design Work

Guidelines in Art

All of us are affected by the world of art and design, but often we are unaware of it. Take for instance the purchase of something quite ordinary — let's say a pair of sun-glasses for the summer. Think for a minute about how you select the right pair.

In front of you, on a rotating rack, you find about fifty different varieties, and usually a little mirror to help you make your choice. What causes you to choose one particular pair over all the others is personal taste, influenced by the image you associate with that particular type of glasses, their colour, their look and how they suit the shape of your face — for indeed most of us are very conscious about what we wear, and this is plainly an interest in fashion.

Such attention to choice illustrates in a small way how each one of us has his/her own unique sense of taste — a clear indication of our individuality.

Fig. 1.2   A selection of sunglasses for the fashion conscious

Marketing personnel are keenly aware of how important it is to accomodate people's various tastes and to please as many people as possible with a single commodity. Be it a brand of margarine or an international superstar, a vast amount of time, energy and money is spent by designers, artists, stylists, etc., in an effort to present the subject to the very best advantage.

These experts know that they must cater to the visual awareness of those they wish to attract and do so by maximising the visual impact and appeal of their creation.

How We see

Shut your eyes ..... there is nothing but darkness; the link with the visible world is severed. Think about this for a moment, then open your eyes again ..... you are now receiving pictures, colours, shapes, dimensions.

The human eye, in its healthy state, is a marvellous piece of engineering and is not unlike the workings of a camera — except that it is vastly more versatile. *Accommodation* is a word used by opticians when discussing the workings of the eye, and it is indeed a very appropriate word, because the eye can adjust to accommodate changes in light intensity, nuances of colour and varying distances.

Within the eyeball is the retina, which is a surface sensitive to colour and light. In front of the retina is a flexible lens which is controlled by ciliary muscles. These muscles control the focusing function of the eye. Directly in front of the lens is the iris, with its muscles which adjust the eye's aperture for light and dark. The iris operates by regulating the size of the pupil, thus allowing the correct amount of light through — *Fig. 1.3.*

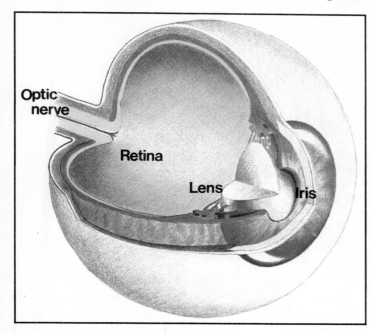

Fig. 1.3

*Artist's representation
of the eye*

Understanding What We See

It cannot be over-emphasised how important it is for the artist to understand his subject. There are people who regard artists as *"being good with their hands"*, almost implying that art does not require intelligence!

Guidelines in Art _____

The professional artist takes an active interest in the workings of what he draws and paints. If, for instance, you are commissioned to do a drawing of a complex shape, such as the engine of a motor car for a car magazine, an understanding of how it works will go a long way towards helping you produce an accurate drawing.

Such understanding ensures that the artist draws the spark plugs directly above the internal combustion chambers, the air filter near the carburettor and so on, so that each part is intelligently placed. This task would be far more tedious if the artist had to rely painstakingly on visual information only.

Another example of this is Life Drawing or Portrait Painting. Here, the artist needs to have an understanding of anatomy. What lies under the skin on the face? How do the muscles work when we laugh, when we shout, etc.? *Fig. 1.4* gives you some idea of this.

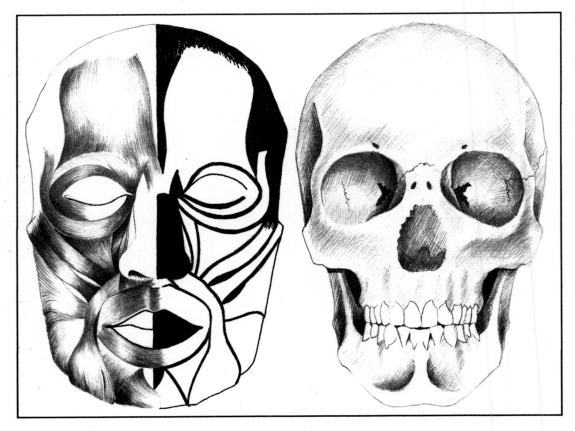

Fig. 1.4   Muscles and bone formation of the face

With understanding and drawing practice, the artist learns to economise. He leaves out those things which are unimportant, so that he can quickly turn out work which is accurate. This is evident in the sketch books of the great masters such as Michaelangelo or Da Vinci. Their sketches were often done very quickly and then taken back into the studio where they were corrected and used for finished work.

Generally, professional artists do not draw everything that they see; instead, they draw only what they consider to be essential. The *camera* records everything in front of it, but the *artist* selects, at his own discretion, what he sees as 'characteristic'. He may place special emphasis on certain aspects of the subject while playing down others. In other words, he interprets his subject in his own unique way, which makes *his* work different from that of all other artists. *Figs. 1.5 & 1.6* illustrate this point well.

Fig. 1.5   Tory Island

Fig. 1.6   Artist James Dixon's impression of the island

Assignment

At your school or local library, find out all you can about the artist Leonardo Da Vinci and write a short note about his life and his most famous painting — the Mona Lisa.

Contour Drawing

Contour drawing is a very beneficial way of training the eye to concentrate. The student follows (with the eye) the outline of what he/she wishes to draw, only occasionally looking down at the page to make slight adjustments. The finished drawing may look a little strange but, nonetheless, the eye will have learned quite a bit from this method. The main thing to remember here is that it is the outline of the subject we are concerned with, and the eye should concentrate only on that. Through this technique, we unlearn the bad habits of drawing which are so common, e.g. childish symbols for features of the face — *Fig. 1.7.*

Fig. 1.7   Look familiar?? Typical attempts at drawing faces!

As children, easy ways of drawing the nose, eyes, etc. were learned and never developed further. Unlearning these symbols is a major step forward in the improvement of our drawing. *Fig. 1.8* shows how we might develop our representation of the human face and its features.

Fig. 1.8   Representation of human face & features

An ideal subject for contour drawing is the human figure. In drawing it as a contour exercise, no attempt at shading should be made, since contour drawing is concerned with the *outline* of the subject only.

13

« Fig. 1.9

Assignment

For one minute only, study either of the two pictures on the left. Then close the book and, from memory, draw what you have seen, including as much detail as possible. Then check your drawing against the original and see how sharp your sense of visual awareness is!

« Fig. 1.10

2 Dimension & Geometrical Shapes

"In nature everything is modelled according to three basic shapes: — the sphere, the cone, the cylinder. We must learn to paint these shapes, then we shall be able to do whatever we wish."
                                                                    Paul Cèzanne

What Is Meant By Dimension?
Dimension is any of the three linear measurements — length, breadth, depth.

Fig. 2.1a shows two parallel lines of a certain length. This is one-dimensional.

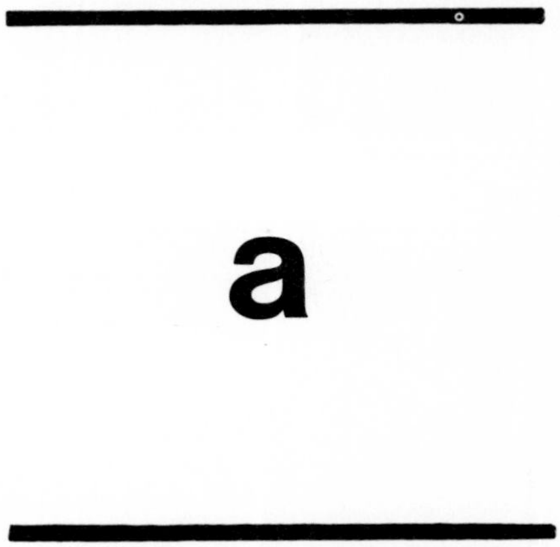

a

Fig. 2.1a

Fig. 2.1b

Fig. 2.1b shows that when two new lines are added, a definite shape can be seen. This is two-dimensional — length & breadth.

Fig. 2.1c shows that by adding extra lines — this time, lines of depth — a third dimension is produced.

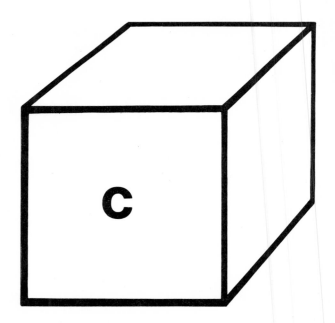

Fig. 2.1c

Three-dimensional (3-D) line drawing can be further enhanced by the addition of light and shade, as seen in the example below.

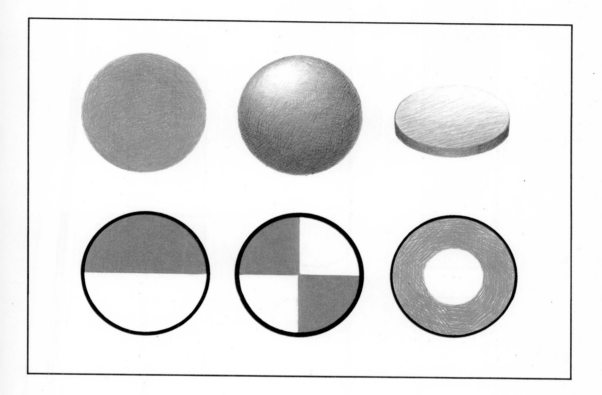

Fig. 2.2   *Working with Light & Shade*

Figs. 2.3 & 2.4 give an idea of how other geometrical shapes can be represented in 3-D, by lines of depth and by light/shade.

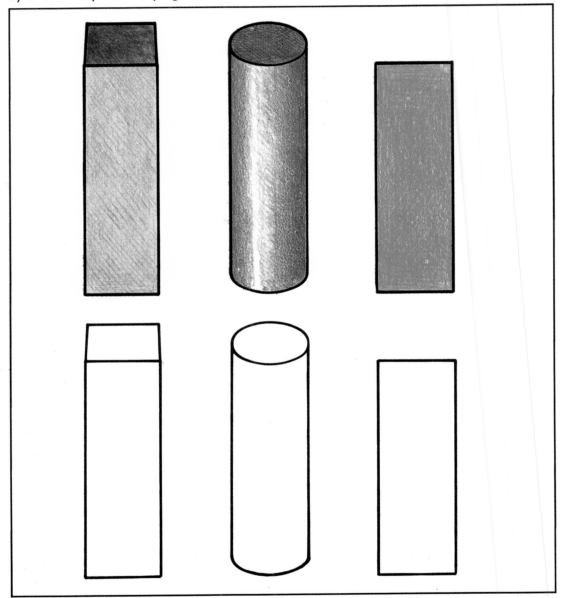

Fig. 2.3   *Blocks and Rods with and without shading*

Fig. 2.4   Pyramidal and Cone shapes in 2-D and 3-D

When you come to study subjects such as Still Life and Life Sketching, you will quickly realize the importance of 3-D drawing. It is the artist's way of representing a 3-D world on a 2-D surface. A page or canvas is flat, so, in itself, it has no bulk or volume, hence the need for methods of 3-D drawing.

Exercise

Taking a large sheet of coloured paper, make up some models of the basic geometric shapes, i.e. rectangles, cylinders, cubes, cones. This will help you to understand what 3-D objects are. Now transfer these shapes (3-D) onto a sheet of white paper (2-D) using a dark pencil and use pencil shading to create a 3-D effect.

3 Elementary Perspective

Perspective is used in painting to create the illusion of space, volume and distance. In architecture and engineering, perspective is an exact science, involving complicated mathematics, but here we need only concern ourselves with the basics. An elementary knowledge will provide us with a means for accurate drawing construction and unusual pictorial composition.

Fig. 3.1 shows a house drawn with no understanding of perspective.

Fig. 3.1

Fig. 3.2 shows the same subject, which has been drawn again, using perspective.

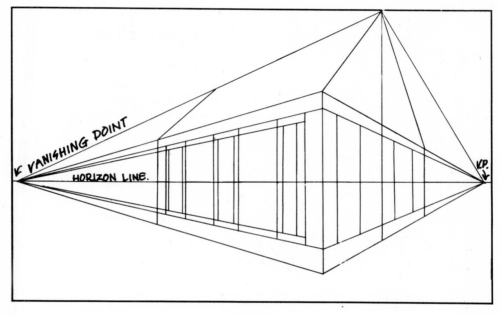

VANISHING POINT

HORIZON LINE.

V.P.

Fig. 3.2

The corrected drawing already looks more convincing. Note that, when making studies of objects for perspective drawing, you must work from a stationary position and view with one eye only.

Guidelines in Art _____

A row of telegraph poles and a railway track are good starting points to illustrate the workings of perspective. In *Fig. 3.3*, notice how the telegraph poles become smaller and smaller in height as they trail off into the distance. The space between the poles becomes smaller too. The spot on the horizon where they disappear is known as *vanishing point*.

Now look at the railway track. It also diminishes in size, until it finally disappears on the horizon. From this, we can see that vertical and horizontal lines decrease in size the further away from the eye they are.

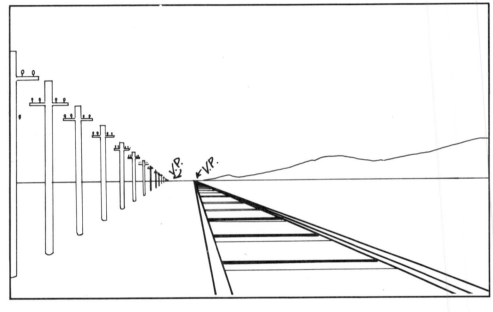

Fig. 3.3

In most pictures there will be a few vanishing points along the horizon, depending on the direction of the lines.

In *Figs. 3.4* and *Fig. 3.5*, other possibilities arise, such as vanishing points which occur both above *and* below the horizon. This situation comes about with planes which slope upwards and downwards — hills and lane-ways for instance. Only those lines which are parallel with level ground have their vanishing points on the horizon.

Fig. 3.4 *Vanishing point below the horizon*

Fig. 3.5 *Vanishing point above the horizon*

23

The Picture Plane

By cutting a 3:5 ratio rectangle from the centre of a piece of stiff black cardboard, a simple view-finder can be made. The ratio of the rectangle should correspond to the page format in use for perspective studies. The viewing window thus made is known as the *picture plane.*

> **Note:** The view-finder should be held stationary in front of one eye and at a fixed distance.

The Horizon Line

The Horizon Line will always be at the eye level of the observer. The horizon may divide a picture at different points. An horizon line can be very low, as in *Fig. 3.6*; mid-way, as in *Fig. 3.7*; or very high, as in *Fig. 3.8*.

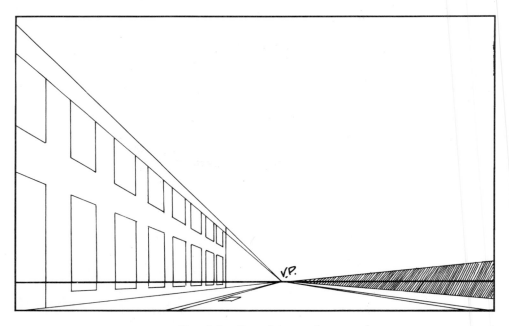

Fig. 3.6   Low horizon line

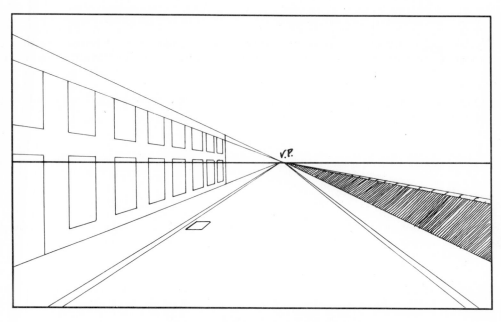

Fig. 3.7   Mid-way horizon line

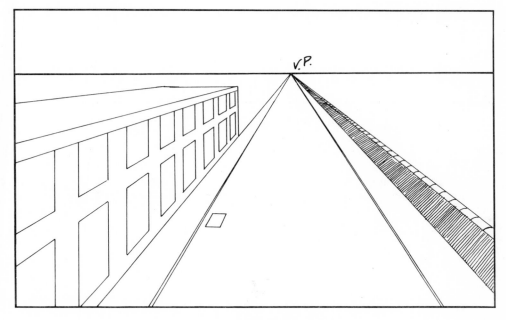

Fig. 3.8   High horizon line

25

The placement of this line depends largely on the angle of view. The low horizon line might be that of a man working in a trench in the ground; the middle horizon that of a man standing upright; the high horizon, a view seen by someone from the top of a tall building.

From high up, we expect to see more landscape than will the man working in the trench. From very low down, we cannot expect to see as much.

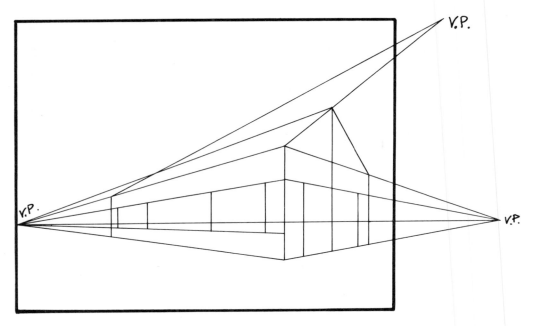

Fig. 3.9   V.P.'s outside of the picture area

In some instances, it may be necessary to extend the horizon line outside the page. Fig. 3.9 shows vanishing points established outside of the picture.

The Vertical Line or Line of Sight

Taking the same example of the railway track and telegraph poles seen in *Fig. 3.3*, a second important line must be established, i.e. the vertical line or line of sight.

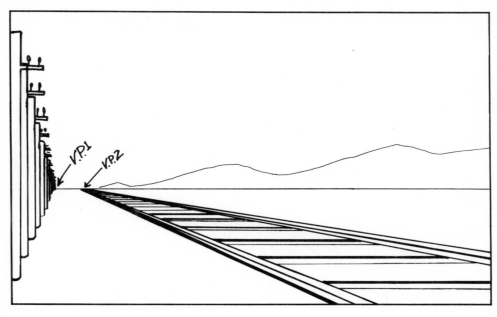

Fig. 3.10

Fig. 3.10 shows what the observer would see if he were to stand further to the left, i.e. nearer the poles.

Fig. 3.11 shows what he would see if he were to move further to the right.

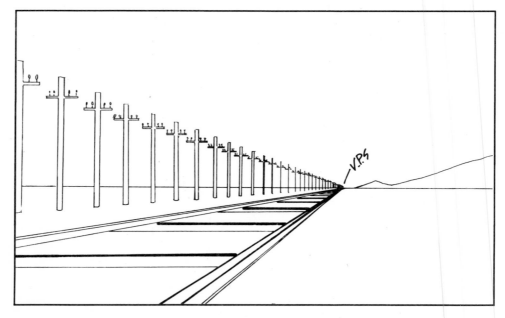

Fig. 3.11

In both *Figs. 3.10 & 3.11*, you will notice that the horizon has not changed, as it is largely affected by the height (or depth) from which the picture is viewed. The line of sight changes, however, when we move from left to right.

When starting a perspective drawing, be it real or imaginary, it is important to establish both of the reference lines mentioned.

Applying Perspective to An Imaginative Composition

In the following examples, you see a room with a tiled floor, a window and a table, which has been drawn from two different angles.

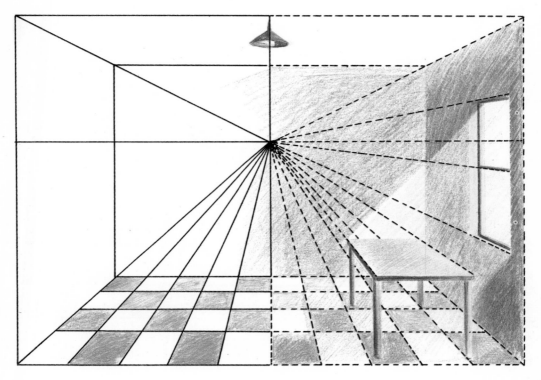

Fig. 3.12

The first example, *Fig. 3.12*, shows the view we would expect to see if we were standing in the middle of the room and looking at the end wall.

The second example, *Fig. 3.13*, shows what we would see if we were lying down on the centre of the floor.

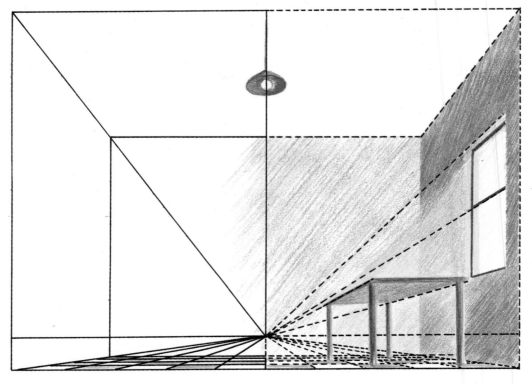

Fig. 3.13

The difference between the two drawings is the changed position of the horizon line.

The following example, *Fig. 3.14*, shows a change in the line of sight, so the position of the vertical line must also change.

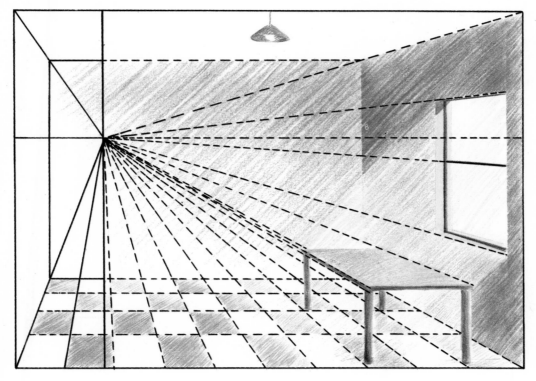

Fig. 3.14

In this drawing, the horizon line does *not* change, as the observer moves from right to left only, and not up or down.

Perspective of Spheres and Circles

No matter what angle a sphere is viewed from, its shape never changes. A football, for instance, may change in size, depending on the distance from which it is viewed, but its shape remains the same (i.e. under no circumstances can it appear oblong or square!).

This is not true of circles, for their shape changes to form ellipses. Drawing an ellipse can be very difficult and very often poses problems, even for professional artists.

The circle can be drawn in perspective — as shown in *Fig. 3.15* —

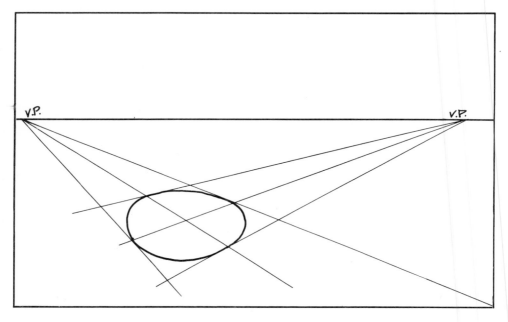

Fig. 3.15

— or by short-cutting perspective rules, as shown in *Fig. 3.16.*

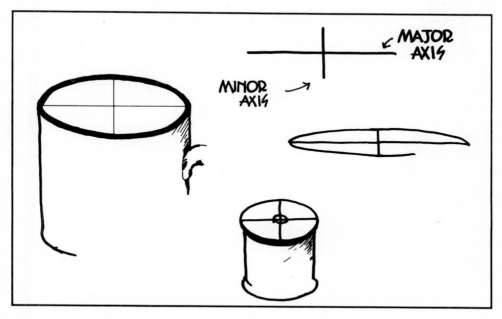

Fig. 3.16

The relative lengths of the major and minor axes are critical if the circle is to form a correct ellipse.

Drawing of the circle should be practised, as it is a recurring feature in Still Life work, e.g. the base of a bottle, the top of a cup, etc.

Fig. 3.17   Cornfield and Cypress Trees ... Vincent Van Gogh

Colour Perspective

The general rule for colour perspective is that warm colours should, in most cases, be painted in the foreground, and cooler ones in the background (*see Fig.4.4, p.47*). Mountains for instance, become more blue in colour the further away they are seen. This is also true of grass, which has a yellowish tint when it is close to us and a bluish colour when it is further away. This is explained by the fact that green is composed of two colours — yellow and blue, (*see Ch. 4*).

In the Van Gogh painting above, careful attention to the use of colour is central to the overall effect of the picture. Note especially the warm/cool colour perspective.

Assignments

1. Draw three boxes, each of which has a different V.P. on the horizon.
2. Having studied the examples in *Figs. 3.12/.13/.14*, try drawing this room from another angle.
3. Study a photograph from a magazine or book which features buildings and trace these to find the Horizon Line, the Vertical Line of Sight and the V.P.'s.
4. Draw (a) a pyramid; (b) a cube; (c) any other geometrical shape, in an imaginary perspective.
5. Using the principles of Colour Perspective, compose a picture and see if these principles really work.
6. Using all you have learned in this chapter about perspective, create a picture using basic shapes — squares, triangles, etc. — which represents an optical illusion.

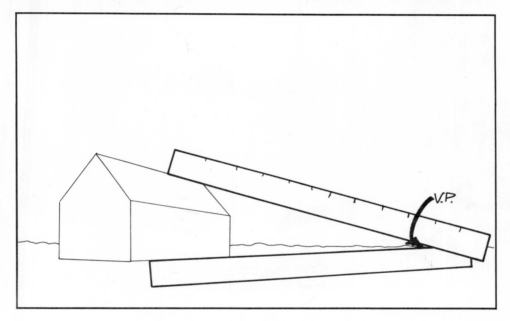

Fig. 3.18

7. In the open country or town, practise establishing V.P.'s of buildings and roads with two rulers, as in *Fig. 3.18*.

N.B. — A Ruler *must* be used in *all* these exercises

35

4 The Principles of Colour

Fig. 4.1   Une Baignade .... Georges Seurat

A fine example of a technique called pointilism, *in which* optical mixing *of colours is used. When viewed from a distance, the tiny dots of colour merge together to give the impression of mixing. Notice how this is done on the blow-up of the bather's cap.*

Before discussing colour, it is first of all necessary to understand something about the nature of light.

Scientists tell us that light is a source of energy, which travels through space in waves, at the phenomenal speed of 186,000 miles per second. These waves are so short that their measurement is expressed in billionths of a metre, or nanometres.

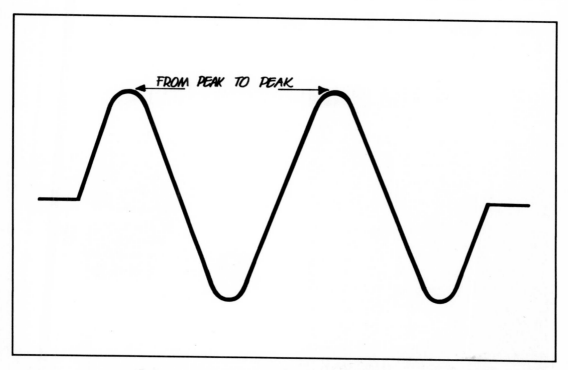

Fig. 4.2   Representation of a light wave. Wavelength may be measured from peak to peak.

The light radiated by the sun is composed of many different wavelengths, some of which are not directly visible to the human eye.

Examples of these invisible waves are Infra Red and Ultra Violet light. In the former, the waves are too long and in the latter, too short, to be picked up by the human eye.

Between the extremes of Infra Red and Ultra Violet however, is a series of waves visible to us. These are the wavelengths of Coloured and White Light, ranging from 400 nanometres to 700 nanometres.

We see White Light, e.g. sunlight, when all the wavelengths in this range are present. If we were to isolate only those waves which are 550 nanometres long, we would see Green Light. Similarly, if we single out *any* one wavelength, we will see the particular colour which corresponds to this wavelength. Therefore, each wavelength between 400 and 700 nanometres produces a specific colour sensation in the eye.

Following rainfall, the White Light of the sun is often split up into a spectrum of colour by the tiny droplets of water in the air, creating what we call a rainbow. This phenomenon shows that White Light is in fact a mix of all the other colours — *Fig. 4.3.*

Fig. 4.3

A Rainbow — white light is separated (dispersed) into its component colours by the prism-like raindrops

Have you ever noticed the amount of people who wear white clothes during summer? In very hot countries, this is even more evident; not only do people *wear* white, but most of their buildings and cars are also white. This has nothing to do with narrowness of taste, but is based purely on common sense. For, when bright sunlight (white light) falls on a white surface, that surface *reflects* (bounces back) waves of all colours. On the other hand, when white light fall on a black surface, the black *absorbs* waves of all colours and then turns this light energy into energy of another form — heat.

This explains why black cars, for instance, become hotter than white cars when exposed to strong sunlight.

In short, white surfaces reflect all light waves; black surfaces absorb all light waves. Thus white makes for coolness in white light (such as sunshine), and black for hotness.

In *Fig. 4.4* we see a ray of White Light with its constituent colour waves (red/orange/yellow/green/blue/indigo/violet) falling on a red surface. All the waves are absorbed *except* the red ones, which are reflected, and are seen by the eye as the colour red.

Fig. 4.4 White Light falling on Red surface

Along with absorption and reflection of waves, our perception of a colour also depends on the effect of neighbouring colours. Despite the fact that there are many colours in the spectrum, there are only 3 pure ones — Red, Green and Blue. They are called Primary colours because they cannot be made by mixing other colours. Rather, all other colours are made by mixing these 3 in different proportions.

****

Light, by its nature, is pure and has a transparent quality. Because of the impurity in paint pigments, however, one alteration in the selection of the primaries has to be made — Yellow is chosen instead of Green. In turn, the Secondary colours of paint differ from those of light and, unlike light, in painting we also have 'tertiary' (or third order) colours. The following section will introduce you to the primary, secondary and tertiary colours of paints.

****

Setting up a Colour Wheel

With a compass, draw a circle of about 6" in diameter and, within this, another circle of 3" diameter. Divide the circumference of this circle into 12 equal parts. This may be done by using a protractor to measure 30° segments — *Fig. 4.5.*

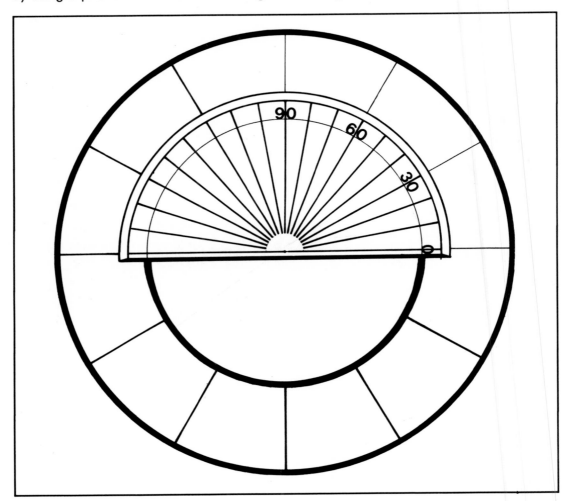

Fig. 4.5   Setting up a colour wheel

When the circumference has been successfully divided, join the markings opposite one another with a line through the centre, and number the segments lightly, with a pencil.

The Primary Colours — 1st order of colour unmixed

With the handle of a teaspoon, or a similar implement, take some red, yellow and blue paint from poster colour jars. Make sure the implement used is properly cleaned each time *before* dipping into a new colour.

Arrange the colours on a mixing palette — as far apart from each other as possible.

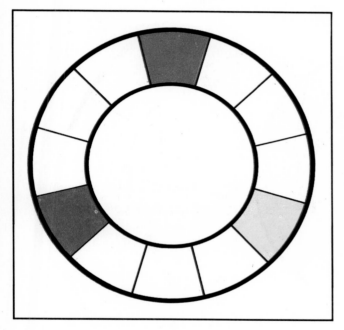

Paint **Red** on segment **1**
Paint **Yellow** on segment **5**
Paint **Blue** on segment **9**

Fig. 4.6

Having done this, we can now turn our attention to mixing new colours on the palette, using the three we have already painted.

The Secondary Colours — 2nd order of colour mixed

Orange   Using a teaspoon, take some **Red** and some **Yellow** paint and mix them well on the palette. This will produce the secondary colour Orange.

Green   Using the cleaned teaspoon again, take some **Yellow** and some **Blue** paint. Mix well on the palette to produce the secondary colour Green.

Violet   Using the cleaned teaspoon, take some **Blue** and some **Red** paint. Mix well on the palette to produce the secondary colour Violet.

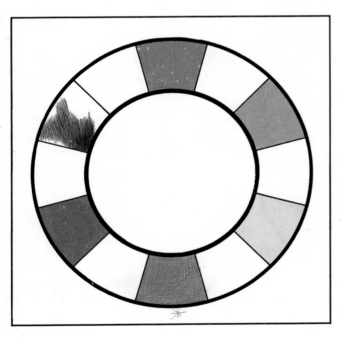

Paint **Orange** on segment **3**

Paint **Green** on segment **7**

Paint **Violet** on segment **11**

Fig. 4.7

Lastly, we can now work with all the colours we have so far painted, to produce a third set of tones.

The Tertiary Colours — 3rd order of colour mixed

The tertiary colours fill in the remaining blank segments on the colour wheel. These are formed on the palette by mixing the primaries with the newly made secondaries.

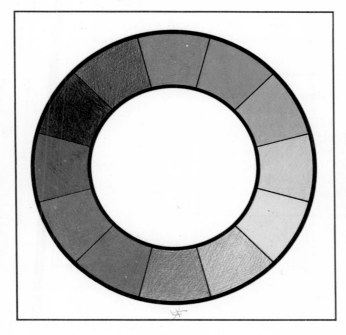

Mix	Paint on
Red & **Orange**	Segment **2**
Yellow & **Orange**	Segment **4**
Yellow & **Green**	Segment **6**
Blue & **Green**	Segment **8**
Blue & **Violet**	Segment **10**
Red & **Violet**	Segment **12**

Fig. 4.8

On completion of this colour mixing exercise, the wheel should show a gradual transition of colour from red to yellow, through to blue, and back again to red. A range of tones has been produced from just 3 colours — *Fig. 4.8.*

Black and White poster paint may be used to darken and lighten these colours. Alternatively, when working on white surfaces, mixtures may be lightened by dilution with water, instead of using white paint. This technique is used by watercolour artists — the white of the page shows through the diluted paint to lighten the colours.

Assignment

Construct another 12-segment wheel. Using black poster paint, paint onto it a range of tones from BLACK through to WHITE. Do not use white paint, but rather dilute the black with water to produce the tonal variations.

Complementary Colours

Colours which appear diametrically opposite each other on the colour wheel are known as Complementary Colours. When placed alongside one another, the effect of these pairs on the eye is visually stimulating.

The following is a selection of complementary pairs:

> **Complementary Pairs**
>
> RED — GREEN
> YELLOW — VIOLET
> ORANGE — BLUE
> VIOLET — YELLOW
> ORANGE/RED — BLUE/GREEN
> RED/VIOLET — GREEN/YELLOW

On *page 45* you can see some applications of complementary colour effects, here using the complementary pair RED — GREEN.

> *N.B.* When complementary colours are mixed they produce Grey.

In *Figs. 4.9, 4.10 & 4.11*, we see the complementary colours Red and Green. Notice the effect caused by these colours. Each colour amplifies the strength of the other, so that they both appear much brighter than they would if seen on their own or next to other colours. Designers, advertising agencies and painters are keenly aware of these relationships between colours and make extensive use of them in their work.

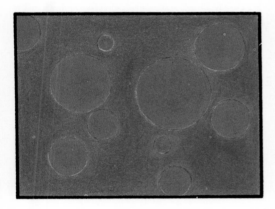

Fig. 4.9   Red/Green design A

Fig. 4.10   Red/Green design B

Fig. 4.11   Traffic Lights
(Colour theory in daily use)

45

More Colour Contrasts

Various other colour contrasts can be created by astute positioning of colours relative to each other.

Light and Dark

Colours of varying brightness will appear brightest when painted alongside dark tones.

Fig. 4.12 shows an example of light/dark contrast — bright blue next to black.

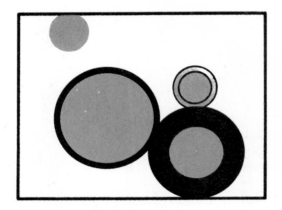

Fig. 4.12 Light/Dark contrast

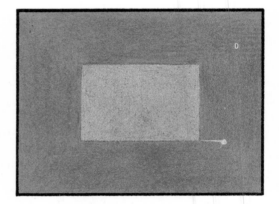

Fig. 4.13 Red/Grey — greenish hue

Simultaneous Contrast

When any colour is painted next to a neutral grey, the grey tends towards the complement of that colour.

Fig. 4.13 shows how red painted adjacent to grey makes the grey seem slightly greenish.

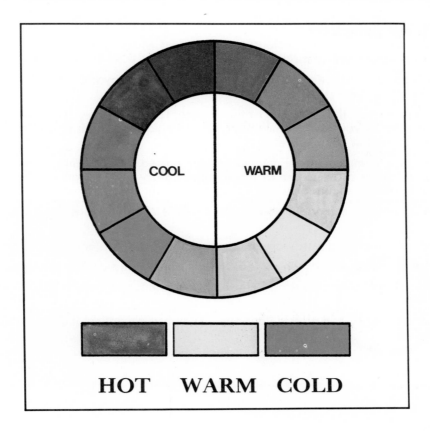

Fig. 4.14   Warm/Cool colour wheel

Warm and Cool Contrast

Fig. 4.14 shows a rough division of the colour wheel into warm and cool colours.

In painting, this contrast can be used to considerable effect. The warm colours will appear warmer still when painted next to the cool ones, and vice-versa.

Guidelines in Art

Assignments

1. In present day fashion, what colours are in vogue? Make notes or sketches from shop windows or magazines to support your views.

2. Using media other than paint (pastels, colour pencils, crayons) make a full range of colours from the three primaries.

3. Study the picture on the first page of this chapter (*Une Baignade ... Georges Seurat*). Now paint a picture of your own choice using this technique (pointilism) and whatever else you have learned in this chapter.

4. In advertising, complementary colours are often used. Take cuttings from magazines, wrappers or boxes showing use of the complementary pair red/green. Try to find one design using these colours only.

5. Using what you have learned about colour in this chapter, work out a weave or knit pattern.

6. Paint colours which suggest: warmth; ice cool; Autumn; Winter.

7. Paint a selection of colours which you find pleasing alongside one another.

8. Create a collage pattern, making full use of all you have learned in this chapter about colour.

9. Working on how colour affects your eyes, compose an optical illusion painting using violet/yellow.

5 Drawing

"Drawing is one of the finest ways of educating the eye, because it involves a concentrated exercise in seeing."

Through the practice of drawing, we have at our disposal an excellent means of investigating and interpreting the visual world. Drawing heightens visual awareness and furnishes the mind with a wealth of ideas. These ideas can be channelled into other areas of art, such as pottery, print design, weaving, painting. It is for this reason that drawing has long been the foundation for many art subjects.

One should not set out with the intention of making *'pretty pictures'* but rather think in terms of carrying out investigative studies of day to day objects. Almost anything is worth drawing — something as ordinary as a shoe-lace can be a worthwhile subject, provided that it is approached with a lively curiosity. This curiosity comes naturally to infants, for the world about them is so new and exciting. Try to redevelop a child's fascination yourself, and see things through fresh eyes.

Before we start using pencils, the following are a number of techniques that will help you with pencil drawing.

Stick drawing

Dip a twig into the some black ink and draw with it. This is a distinctive technique very suitable for contour drawing.

Chalk and black paper

Using a sheet of black sugar paper, take some coloured chalk and draw with it — make use of the sides and point of the chalk to create different effects.
  This technique is particularly useful for Gesture Drawings of the figure or for introducing light and shade into Figure Drawing or Still Life.

Drawing with Paint

Drawing with paint can make you feel more free in your drawing. Paint drawings can be done with different size paint brushes, with strips of cardboard or even with the fingers.

Pencils

Pencils are very suitable tools for drawing, as they come in a variety of grades, are inexpensive, and a sharp point can be easily maintained.

At least five different grades should be bought —**2H / H /HB / B / 2B**. *Fig. 5.1* shows the different tones produced by this selection.

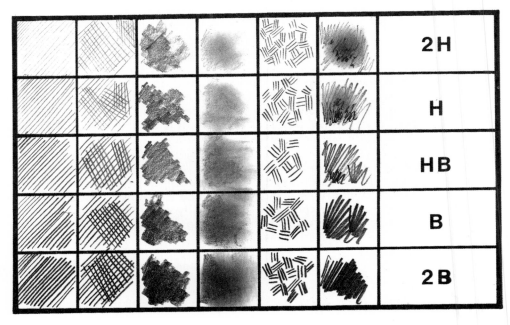

Fig. 5.1   Pencil shadings

Pencils should be topped (sharpened) with a craft knife or similar cutting device. Avoid using short pencils, as control will be restricted.

Erasers

When purchasing an eraser, make sure that it is made of rubber; plastic erasers can cause smudging.

Paper

It is important not to overlook the fact that paper is also a drawing medium. Papers come in a variety of grades and grains, and produce different effects. Never draw heavily onto paper, as its attractive grained surface will be ruined and errors will be difficult to correct.

Many students restrict experimentation with drawing for fear of wasting paper. To avoid this, the use of cheap paper (e.g. newsprint) is advisable for rough work. Better quality papers, such as cartridge type, can be used for finished pieces; this type of paper will also take poster colour and water colour washes successfully.

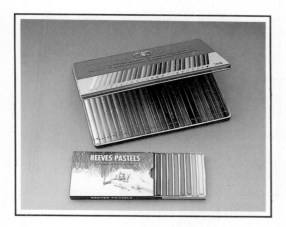

Fig. 5.2

Coloured pencils & pastels suitable for sketching onto paper

Considerations When Drawing

Shadows

Shadows should always be drawn carefully, as they provide clues to shapes, and are useful compositional aids.

Folds

Folds — such as those found in garments, table cloths, etc. — help us to define form or shape, and give dimension to a drawing.

Assignment

Wrap a model in a white sheet, creating lots of folds in the material. Then, using a direct light source, draw the shape of the body, concentrating on the lines of the folds.

Guidelines in Art

Light

Make good use of light, as it governs shadows and the illumination of objects.

Assignment

Using a direct light source, e.g. a side lamp, draw a group of Still Life objects. Darken the room so that there are areas of direct light and shade.

Fig. 5.3

The Carpenter's Household ... Rembrandt

Note here the artist's use of light & shade, the stream of light from the window controlling the whole focus of the piece.

Negative Shape

Fig. 5.4 shows what a negative shape is. By studying such shapes, and drawing them, the eye is forced to see things afresh. In painting and drawing, negative shapes are as important as positive (i.e. directly visible) shapes.

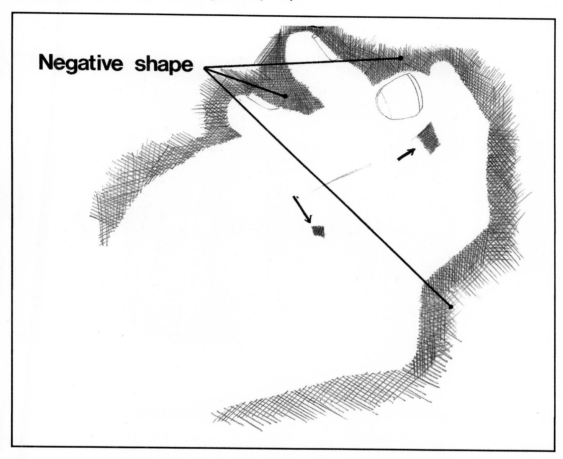

Fig. 5.4

Store Information

Before attempting to draw anything, you should study both its negative and positive shapes. Many students, when drawing, seldom look up from the page. It is important to make frequent comparisons between your work and what it is you are drawing.

Angle of the drawing board

Ideally this should be tilted at an angle of 45°.

Geometrical Shapes

Be conscious of the underlying geometrical forms (rectangular, circular, cylindrical, etc.) in your subject.

Assignment

Draw some Still Life objects, breaking them down into their basic geometric shapes, and shade them to create a 3-D effect.

Proportion

Proportion can be measured with a pencil, as in *Fig. 5.5*.

Fig. 5.5   Studying proportion using a pencil

It is essential that the arm be kept straight for each measurement taken.

Detail Drawing

Detail drawing involves taking a small area of, say, a leaf, and drawing it in as much detail as possible, over a period of an hour or so. Never tackle something too big, as this will take a lot of time, and will inevitably try your patience. Select such things as a small piece of drift wood, an ink bottle, a watch — i.e. something small and detailed. This type of study should be worked on cartridge paper, using hard pencil grades, such as 2H or H.

Assignment

In your school or local library try to locate a picture of Rubens' *Study of Cows* and observe its wealth of detail.

Swift and Undetailed Drawing (Gesture Drawing)

This type of study should be carried out very quickly, in order to get the feel of the drawing. Lines which overshoot and cross each other in all sorts of ways usually result and there is no need to erase them — remember it is only a "warm up" phase. Make several such drawings on cheap paper.

Assignment

For fine examples of this kind of drawing have a close look at Degas' *Dry Brush Sketches — from Originals* and Rembrandt's *Sketch of a Girl Sleeping*.

Economy Line Drawing

This type of drawing can be very difficult, despite its apparent simplicity. As only those lines which characterise the subject should be drawn, a discriminating eye is called for. Each line or mark on the page must add to the finished piece.

Fig. 5.6

— Lionesses —
Gaudier Brzeska

Notice the spontaneity and the uncluttered simplicity of pure line drawing in this piece of artwork.

Assignment

In your school or local library, locate David Hockney's *Henry with Cigar* or Picasso's *Three Dancers*, two fine examples of economy line drawing.

Figure Drawing

The ability to draw figures convincingly only comes about through much practice. Proportion is most likely to be the greatest problem. *Figs. 5.7 & 5.8* show how the human body is broken down into divisions. Learn these divisions.

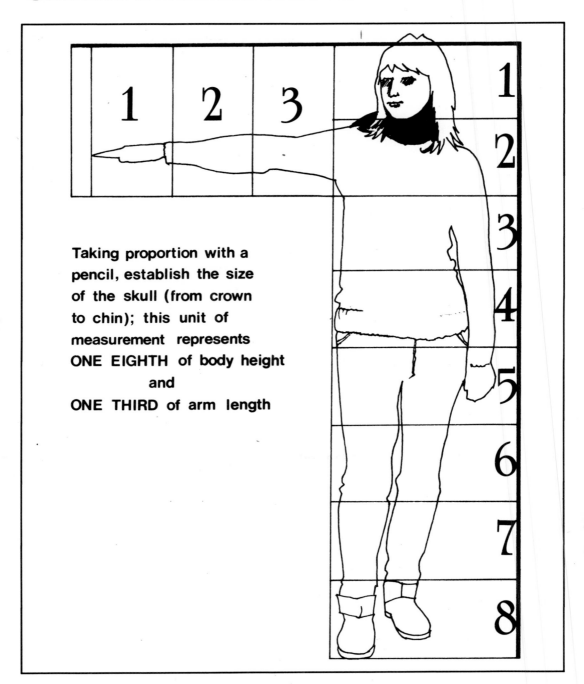

Taking proportion with a
pencil, establish the size
of the skull (from crown
to chin); this unit of
measurement represents
ONE EIGHTH of body height
              and
ONE THIRD of arm length

Fig. 5.7   Divisions of the human form

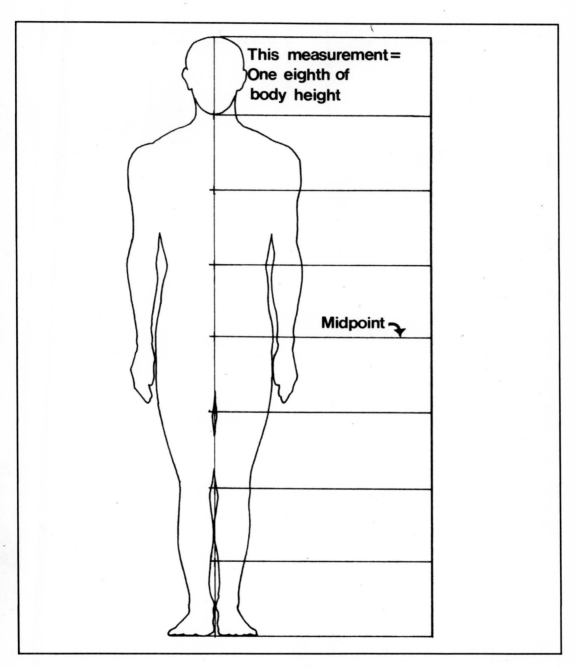

This measurement =
One eighth of
body height

Midpoint

Fig. 5.8   Divisions of the human form

Fig. 5.9

*The correct way to hold a pencil
for Gesture Drawing
(movement of the whole arm)*

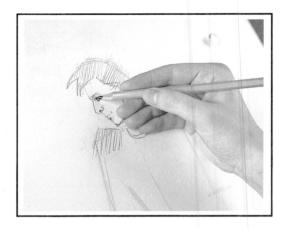

Fig. 5.10

*The correct way to hold a pencil
for Detail Drawing
(hand movement only)*

It will not always be possible to draw from life, so it is recommended that you also copy figure shapes from photographs, comics and magazines.

When drawing from life, do a few quick undetailed studies first. During this time the model will have settled into a pose. (Models tend to move a little for the first few minutes until they find a relaxing position.)

When sketching, seat yourself in a position where the scale of the subject suits the page size. This can be checked by taking proportion measurements, with a pencil, as shown earlier (*Fig. 5.5*).

Fig. 5.11   Figure & Schemata

Schemata are helpful when establishing posture on the page; they also give an idea of how much page space the drawing will finally occupy. Avoid drawing too small or too big.

Remember to check scale and proportion, as already explained.

In the case of a standing posture, a vertical line must be established. This line runs from the top of the head down to the foot which carries the most weight. It is less common for a model to stand with the weight equally distributed. If this is the case, however, the vertical line falls between the two feet — *Fig. 5.12*. On this line, we fix reference points where the divisions of the body occur and to indicate how wide the body frame will be — *Fig. 5.13 & 5.14*.

Fig. 5.12

The vertical line is not always straight, however, as illustrated — *Figs. 5.13 & 5.14*.

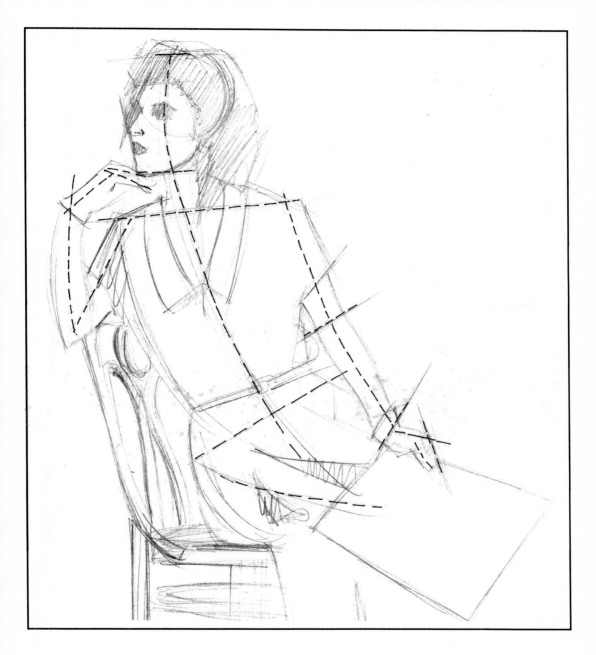

Fig. 5.13

Fig. 5.14

Foreshortening

When drawing figures, it is not uncommon to come across poses where the model has a limb, such as a leg or a hand, extended. If the extended limb is nearer to the artist than the rest of the body, problems of foreshortening will arise.

Foreshortening brings with it changes in proportion. For instance, an artist drawing a model who is seated with one leg extended, will most likely draw the extended leg larger than the other, to give the impression that it is nearer.

A model may also be seated in such a way that the head leans forward. In this case, therefore, it is the head which will be drawn larger than normal.

Assignment

At your school or local library, study David Hockney's *Joe Mc Donald*, paying particular attention to the foreshortening technique.

Hands

Cover the surface area of your face with one hand and note the size relationship between face and hand.

As a general rule, a hand which is open, fully occupies the same space as the surface area of the face. This is a useful tip when trying to establish the proportion of hands in relation to the rest of the body, since students very often make the mistake of drawing hands too small in relation to the rest of the body.

The Head

Many students are fascinated by portraiture (i.e. drawing of the head) which can indeed be a challenging and rewarding study, as it is for many professional artists.

Fig. 5.15   Portraiture

Fig. 5.16

Portraiture

Guidelines in Art

The newcomer to portraiture should not be preoccupied with *"getting a likeness"*, as this will certainly lead to a great deal of discouragement. Achieving a likeness requires a lot of practice and patience.

For the beginner, familiarity with different head shapes, eyes, noses, ears, etc. should be a first priority. Ability to draw a likeness will follow later.

Figs. 5.17, 5.18 & 5.19 show a head drawn from different angles, with proportion references.

NOTE THE CURVATURE OF THESE LINES AS THEY FOLLOW THE ROUND SURFACE OF THE SKULL —

① — DETERMINE SKULL SHAPE AND MARK IN GUIDELINES FOR THE POSITIONS OF THE NOSE, EYES ETC. —

② — NEXT THE HAIR OUTLINE AND DRAW IN THE FEATURES ROUGHLY —

③ — REMOVE GUIDELINES AND REFINE THE DRAWING. —

Fig. 5.17

Drawing the head

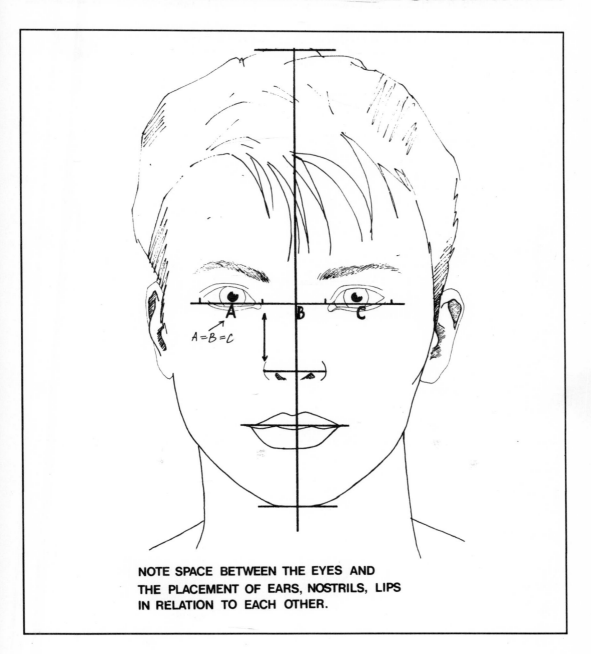

A = B = C

NOTE SPACE BETWEEN THE EYES AND
THE PLACEMENT OF EARS, NOSTRILS, LIPS
IN RELATION TO EACH OTHER.

Fig. 5.18

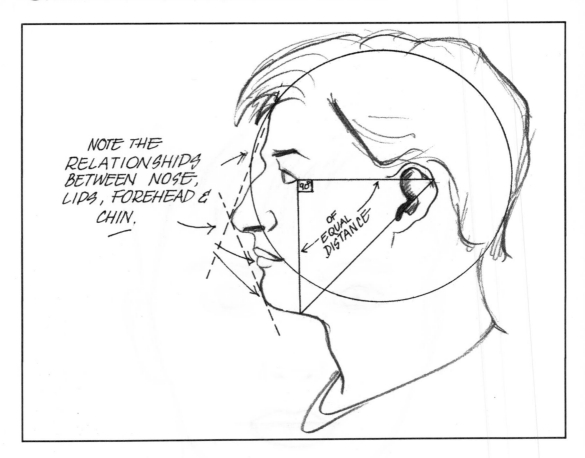

Fig. 5.19

Assignment

Make a head from Papier Maché using a balloon for the basic shape, then building up areas of the face, nose, mouth, eyes, chin, etc. — this will help you to better understand head and face structures.

Figure Subjects and Surroundings

Fig. 5.20
Girl Sewing ... John Coyle

The introduction of a chair or another familiar object is a good idea when figure drawing, as it helps to relate the figure to its surroundings and can furthermore be useful as a compositional device. *Fig. 5.20* above illustrates this point well.

Guidelines in Art

Practical Assignments relating to the Figure

1. 3-Dimensional Ideas

Using strong wire, make an armature to show a certain body position, e.g. standing with feet together and one arm out to the side. Then, using fine flexible wire or pipe cleaners, build up the body. You should concentrate on its general shape and 3-D quality rather than on specific details.

1. Detailed Modelling

(a) More detailed modelling can be done using clay, which is then fired in a kiln and glazed. Note that interesting textures, e.g. hair & clothes, can be quite easily modelled in clay.

(b) Papier Maché and chicken wire can produce interesting effects, and old clothes can be used to make a figure more realistic — shoes, wigs, jeans, T-shirts, jackets, and so on.

(c) Plaster can also be used and, in combination with the other materials mentioned, allows full life-size figures to be modelled, e.g. when undertaking theme projects — models of: a rugby team; a night at a disco; waiting for the bus; etc. Such work allows you to concentrate on a study of different positions.

3. Stylised Life Drawing

Take time to study various styles of drawing — anything from fashion design to record covers and book illustration. Examine the work of such artists as Jim Fitzpatrick and James Dean. Then, design your own fashions, record covers, story books, etc.

6 Composition

Fig. 6.1   Tuscany ... Carey Clarke

Composition is essential in all facets of art. It is the method by which elements, or parts, are arranged into an organised and pleasing whole.

In story writing, the author employs composition to hold the reader's attention. Each episode in the narrative is designed to convey certain information which is relevant to the overall purpose of the story. The author will attempt to give sufficient information to keep the reader interested, while at the same time, perhaps, reserving the most important disclosure until the last pages. Unnecessary digressions will confuse the reader and may cause him/her to lose all interest in the story.

Pictorial composition, be it from imagination or from reality, warrants the same careful consideration. Use all possible means to lead the viewer's eye to the centre of interest or the *focal point*. Every line or colour on the page is of consequence as it may add to, or take from, the finished piece. You should experiment freely, therefore, as good compositional sense comes mainly from practice.

Notice the way the table in the forground cleverly leads the viewer's eye to the vacant seat. From this point the eye then scans from left to right.

*

Fig. 6.2   L'Absinthe ... Edgar Degas

Looking at the works of Degas and Manet, shown in *Figs. 6.2 & 6.3*, notice how in each of these works, the artist directs the onlooker's gaze and holds his interest. Nothing in the paintings is superfluous. Every shape adds to the finished whole.

Fig. 6.3   Früstuck im Auteuer ... Eduard Manet

Suggestions For Pictorial Composition

1. Do not divide a picture into two equal divisions; this can be difficult to control, even for accomplished artists.

2. Simplify complex shapes into patterns which are easy to handle.

3. Use artistic licence. If you feel that something is best left out or its position altered, do this, provided you are *sure* it benefits the composition.

4. Remember that shadows and negative shapes are just as important as the visible objects and may also be used to aid composition.

5. Perspective can be used to great advantage when planning a composition. Vertical and horizontal reference lines will give a reasonable idea of the main centre of emphasis and interest.

6. The introduction of a figure, in real or imaginative townscapes or landscapes, gives an idea of scale and adds interest.

7. Avoid drawing roads or laneways which lead out of the picture. Alter their direction if you think it helps the composition.

8. To create a well balanced picture, you can use a traditional rule known as the *Intersection of Thirds*. This principle works as follows:

Using a pencil, lightly, divide the page, both horizontally and vertically, into 3 equal sections. The points at which the lines cross each other are known as the *intersection of thirds*. At any one (or sometimes more than one) of these points, the main subject, e.g. face(s), house(s), etc., should be located.

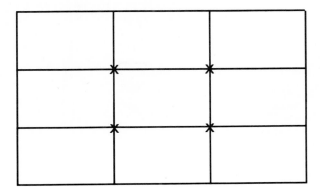

One should not adhere to this principle for all pictorial composition, as the resulting artwork would, inevitably, be monotonously similar. Nonetheless, when used with due discretion, it is a viable working formula.

9. Composition of colour plays a very important role *(see Chapter 3)*.

10. Make maximum use of light and shade.

Exercise

Compose a picture based on one of the following:

The Shoemaker	The Video-Game Player	
The Excavation	Strawberry Fields	A Poem of your choice from your
Tourists	At the Pottery	Irish or English language Courses.
The Nightclub	The Window-Shoppers	

7 Painting

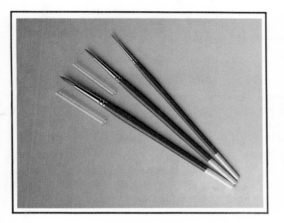

Fig. 7.1   Imitation sable-haired brushes
*These are relatively inexpensive and
of good quality*

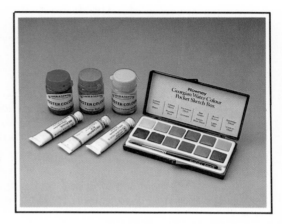

Fig. 7.2   Selection of paints
Poster colours and water colours

Preparation of Paper

When working with water-based paint, paper should be stretched, if time permits. This practice will prevent buckling of the page when moistened. The following is a description of how paper may be stretched.

The paper is first soaked in a bath of clean water, for about five minutes; then it is placed on a drawing board and fastened down with gum backed tape — *Fig. 7.3*. Allow the paper to dry for about six hours, by which time it will be taut and even. As paper stretching takes a lot of time, it is advisable to stretch a few sheets at a time, on different boards, for later use.

Fig. 7.3

Stretching paper with gum-backed tape

An alternative but less effective method of painting onto paper is simply to fasten the paper to a drawing board with four thumb tacks. This is quick and far less troublesome than paper stretching, but the page will buckle a little when paint is applied.

Painting is an extension of drawing. The student who has developed his/her drawing ability will find that painting comes quite easily. Rushing the drawing stage of a piece of work so as to *"get on with"* the painting stage is a failing common to many students of art. Remember that a well executed drawing makes for a better painting.

Painting, of course, is much concerned with colour and a keen visual awareness in this regard is an asset to any painter.

Fig. 7.4   Colour patterns from disco lights

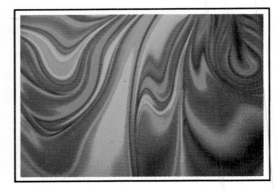

Fig. 7.5   Colour patterns of a soap bubble

Monochrome Painting

Monochrome is an ideal introduction to painting as it requires the use of only one colour. This type of painting frees the artist to practise tonal variation, handling of the brush, and the application of paint.

Fig. 7.6   Dawn, Killarey Bay ... Paul Henry
(Courtesy of the Ulster Museum)

Fig. 7.6 above, although not strictly a monochrome painting, shows what can be achieved using various tones of blue.

Painting in Colour

As you are aware, a great variety of colour can be mixed from the the three primaries and black/white. Always keep this in mind during your painting exercises.

Fig. 7.7   *Convent Garden, Brittany ... W.J.Leech*
(*Courtesy of The National Gallery, Dublin*)

In this painting notice how the artist uses relatively few colours to great effect.
Impressions are achieved by variation of tones and by a most effective use of light.

Mix colours to match those you see before you, rather than resorting to approximate ready-mixed colours. There is a vast selection of colours to choose from in most art shops, but at the early stages the student should confine him/herself to a limited selection, until his/her mixing ability develops. Mixing should always be done on a palette or saucer and *not* in the jar or at the tip of the tube. It is essential also that brushes be cleaned thoroughly after use and stored in a small roll of corrugated cardboard.

For the more advanced student, a list of additional colours is given below. These are popular favourites with many artists, each pigment having its own distinctive flavour and charm.

Cadmium Yellow	Coerileum	Crimson Alizarin	Burnt Umber
Yellow Ochre	Ultra Marine Blue	Rose Madder	Raw Umber
Raw Sienna	Cobalt Blue	India Red	Burnt Sienna
Viridian	Lamp Black	Vermillion	Ivory Black

Making use of Complementary Colour in a Picture

As we have seen in *Chapter 3*, colours which lie diametrically opposite to each other on the colour wheel increase their mutual intensity when painted adjacent to one another.

Many artists like to use one dominant colour as the basis for a given painting. Sub-dominant colours in the painting tend to be complementary of the main colour. This method enhances the intensity of colour within the picture. If you decide to use this method, do not be too direct in your approach, e.g. stark red/green pictures. Working, for instance, with a green based painting — a landscape perhaps — you could introduce subtle red based complementary tones, e.g. purples, violets, oranges.

A cleverer way still of introducing the complement is the painting of a grey backdrop (sky or pavement, perhaps). The eye sees the complement of the adjacent colour in the grey.

Fig. 7.8

In the Greenhouse ... Brett Mc Entagart

Notice the effective use of complementary colouring in this green based piece

Fig. 7.9

Moore Street Market ... N. D'Ardia Caracciolo

Once again, notice the arrangement of complements.

Other Contrasts

Light & Dark Tones

Make use of light and dark tones in a picture *(see Chapter 4)* to highlight points of interest. A bright sun will only appear bright if painted against a suitable sky colour — *Fig. 7.10, not* as in *Fig. 7.11*. Remember, the brightest white available to you is that of the paper on which you are drawing. Note: Usually, the backround should be painted first.

Fig. 7.10

Fig. 7.11

Fig. 7.12

Analogous or Harmonious Colour

Instead of using contrasting colours, you can also experiment with colours of the same family, e.g. reds, violets and purples; or yellows, oranges, ambers; and so on. Colours which lie adjacent to each other on the colour wheel are said to be *analogous* or *harmonious.*

Artwork which makes use of harmonious colouring will probably be more serene, or less 'tense', than that based on contrasting colours.

> **Note:** Always work from light to dark.

81

Painting a Wash

Figs. 7.13 & 7.14 show how to paint a wash of colour. Note the angle of the drawing board, which allows the first line of paint applied to run into the next line painted, and so on until the whole page is covered with an even coat of colour.

Fig. 7.13

Fig. 7.14

Creating Textures with Paint

1. Using a hard paint brush, push the bristles of the brush onto the paper and note the effect — this can be used when painting trees, grass, etc.
2. Using a small paint brush, make bristles work like strokes on a page — what could this be used for?
3. Using the side of a ruler, pull paint along a page and note the effect created.
4. Using a tooth-brush charged with paint, create a spray effect. This can also be achieved with a can of spray paint or with an air brush.
5. Create your own textured effects with paint. These can all be used to make your painting more interesting.

Note: Paint can be applied either thickly or thinly. Ideally the student should opt for one style or the other. For instance, when working with water colours, where thin dilute washes are used, it would be most inappropriate to ruin the delicacy of this style by applying a blob of thick paint!

Still Life

Still life has long been regarded as a fundamental exercise in painting. It provides the opportunity to study the form, light/shade and colour of objects which are stationary. Almost any static object or group of objects is suitable for Still Life study.

How to Approach Still Life Painting

Select a small variety of objects, keeping form, colour and texture in mind. Place these, in an organised manner, on a table approximately eight feet away from your working position (the size of the objects will dictate the exact distance). In order to keep your drawing in proportion, it helps if you tilt your drawing board at an angle of 45°.

It is very important to make a few preliminary sketches in order to *"get the feel"* of the subject matter. *Figs. 7.15 & 7.16* show how one artist went about constructing his picture.

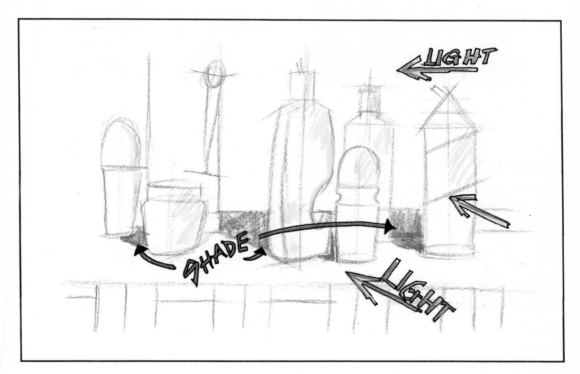

Fig. 7.15

Fig. 7.16

Note: When working on a painting, pay attention to the relative sizes of the objects in view and how much space they will finally occupy on the page. Be aware also of the direction of light, shadows, negative shapes, etc. — as discussed in *Chapter 3.*

Assignments

Proportion

Select a group of Still Life objects. Using coloured paper, cut out the shapes which occur in this group. Pay special attention to the relationship of each shape to the others around it. Finally, place your cut-outs in the same order on the page as they appear in the selected composition, over-lapping them as appropriate.

Texture

Let one member of the class pick up one of the objects in the Still Life group and with his/her eyes closed, feel and describe to the class the various textures of the object. Then let each member of the class individually select an object, feel it blindly and then write a brief description of its shape and texture.

8 Printmaking

There are many different methods of printmaking, some of which are quite basic, while others require considerable skill, forward planning and consideration. The more basic techniques go back to earliest times when they were first used to print patterns on cave walls and later on textiles and parchment. Prehistoric man was certainly aware, as he walked on soft surfaces such as sand, that he left footprints, or impressions, behind. He probably experimented by making other impressions with leaves and twigs. Indeed, early man extended his hunting skills by identifying the footprints that various animals left behind.

With the development of the written word and the eventual spread of literacy, the need for a printing technique became apparent. The first printed books were made by hand carving the letters for each page on wooden printing blocks, inking them and pressing them onto a suitable surface — this was very slow and expensive work.

All changed, however, in 1450, when Johann Gutenberg, from Mainz, developed the first printing press which used movable type. Instead of carving out a whole page of written matter, he made several moulds of the same letter. These letters could then be assembled in a frame, to form a complete page of writing, suitable for printing. When the printing was finished, the letters could be disassembled and reassembled to form yet another page of print.

These great advances in printing paved the way for many of today's modern printing techniques. Since artists were often required to illustrate books, the technique of printing became an art form in itself, with the use of etching, screen printing, etc. This chapter examines a few basic printing techniques, some of which date back to the earliest days of printing.

Impression Prints

Using a light grade paper (e.g. air mail paper), an impression print can be made. Place the paper on a reasonably hard and textured surface and rub over it lightly with a grade HB pencil, held sideways. Very soon the underlying textured pattern will reveal itself on paper — *Fig. 8.1.*

Fig. 8.1

This type of print is very useful for examining both natural and synthetic patterns. It is advisable to carefully store away such prints as reference material for other art studies.

Monoprints

Monoprinting, as the name suggests, involves producing just one print from a master design. This kind of printing, therefore, though very attractive, is unsuited to repeating patterns, such as wallpaper designs.

Monoprinting is best done with a roller and a small sheet of glass — *Figs. 8.2 & 8.3*. Spread a thin coat of printing ink on the glass. It is advisable to place a stiff piece of cardboard under the glass, lest it should break under pressure when making the print. Now, with your finger, paint brush or pencil, draw various patterns on the inked glass, so that different effects are created. When the design has been completed, clean your hands thoroughly. (Cleanliness is very important in printing!) You are now ready to make the first Monoprint.

Carefully place a sheet of clean white paper on the inked surface, and apply even pressure all over (a clean printer's roller is very suitable for this). Now lift the paper slowly to reveal the print.

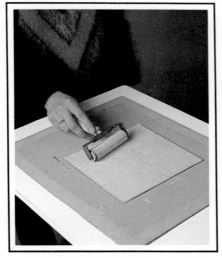

Fig. 8.2   Inking a sheet of glass for monoprinting with a print roller

Fig. 8.3   Monoprint in green

Vegetable Prints

Prints can also be made from vegetables. Ideally the chosen vegetable should be firm — carrots or onions for instance. To make a print, cut the vegetable through the centre in one even cut, so that the exposed inside surface is level for printing. This surface is then inked with a printing roller, sponge or soft material. Again, take care not to over-ink the printing surface or blobbing will result. Press the inked surface firmly against a clean sheet of paper. A print will result, showing the fibrous pattern of the vegetable.

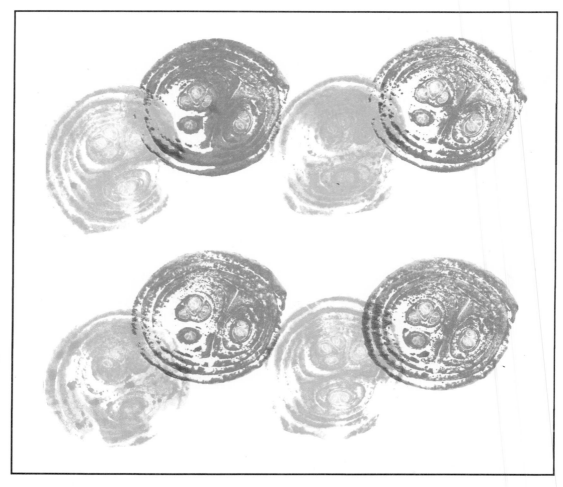

Fig. 8.4   Onion print in two colours

By re-inking, many more prints can be made. Try different colours. Rule a page into squares which accommodate the vegetable print and create a repeating pattern — *Fig. 8.4.*

Relief Printing

Potatoes can be used for printing, but will not produce any fancy fibre patterns of their own, as the cut surface is rather smooth and unpatterned. To make a potato print, first cut the potato through the centre, and then, using a craft knife, or some other suitable cutting implement, carve out a design or motif on the surface. (Remember, only the surface which stands out will print — this surface is called a *relief.*) Ink the relief with the printing roller and make a print.

Fig. 8.5   Potato relief print

It can be interesting also to try a two-tone print, inking with two different colours on separate parts of the relief surface.

You can also ink leaves and other suitably surfaced objects. Relief printing (using wood-cuts) was used to print the first books.

Lino Cuts

Lino cutting is another form of relief printing. However, it requires more cutting skill, preparatory work and practice with special cutting tools.

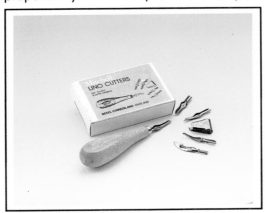

Fig. 8.6

Lino cutting tools

The lino and tools are not expensive and can be purchased at any good art store. When selecting lino, it is advisable to choose a pale colour, so that the design outline, later to be drawn on its surface (for carving), can be easily seen.

Preliminary Practice

Take a small piece of lino and cut some grooves on the surface with the different cutting tools. These grooves should not be cut too deep — ideally ½ the thickness of the lino. From doing this, you will soon realize that a lot of practice is required before attempting complicated work. Ink the lino and make a print. Place the lino carefully on a sheet of paper, ensuring that it does not shift under pressure; if it does, double images or blobs will result. Lift the lino block to reveal the print.

As with all printing methods, there will be failures, but failing is one of the best ways of realizing the limitations of a medium. Keep your Lino Cut designs as simple as possible, however.

Making A Design Suitable for Lino Cutting

Make several sketches of something simple, e.g. a floral pattern, on light quality paper (best for tracing). Each sketch should be a further step in simplification, until you are finally convinced that the design is suitable for carving on lino. Remembering that the lino carving should be in reverse (so that it prints the right way around), trace the final design onto the lino with carbon paper.

When the tracing is finished, you are ready to commence the lino cutting. It is possible to make a print half-way through the cutting stage, to monitor progress, but this is not recommended, as the printing ink residue often darkens the lino surface, and the outline of the design becomes hard to see.

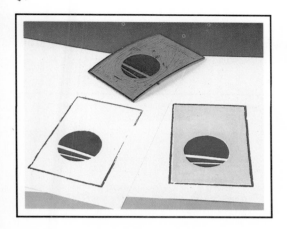

Fig. 8.7

At top of picture, the lino used to print blue/yellow lino cut pattern with blue border (seen at bottom of picture)

Borders

Fig. 8.7 shows a lino cut. As this design stands out in the centre only, and the surrounding material has been carved away, it is necessary to leave a raised border at the edge of the lino. This will prevent the printing of the now thin and weakened edges. The border is essential when working on larger lino prints. This border will print along with the design, but it can be cut off when the print is dried. A further advantage of the border is that it makes registration easy when overlaying with a separate lino cut (two-colour prints). The border of the second lino can be positioned accurately on the printed border of the first lino.

Fig. 8.8   *Green/yellow and Blue/yellow combination prints*

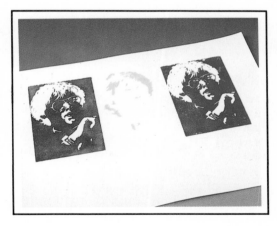

Fig. 8.9   *Green, yellow & blue prints from which combinations were made. Note: the white paper is used as an extra colour.*

Printing in More than One Colour

Some linos are supplied ready-mounted on wooden blocks which reinforce them; this eliminates the need for a border — *Fig. 8.10.*

Fig. 8.10

Photo, design and block for lino prints on previous page.

It is preferable that the lino block for each colour to be printed should be the same size, so that the registering of the second print is made easier.

Stencil Prints

By making paper cut-outs, it is easy to create simple stencil prints. The cut-out is placed on a sheet of clean paper and paint or ink is sprayed over it. Spraying is best done with an aerosol, but a toothbrush charged with paint can also be used — *Fig. 8.11.*

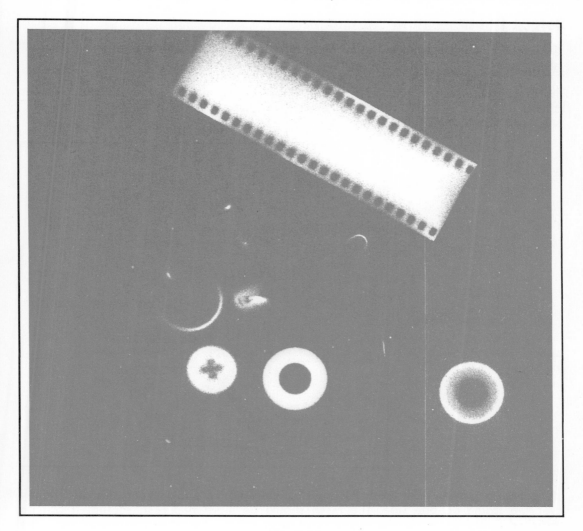

Fig. 8.11

Heavy quality paper is most suitable for making the stencil, as lighter grades tend to curl once moistened with paint.

It is interesting also to experiment with readily available stencils, such as sycamore leaves, blades of grass, etc. Placing paper underneath, spray over different shapes, to explore some of the possibilities.

Screen Prints

Silk screen printing is used in the fabric printing trade and in poster printing.

Making The Screen

The first requirement is a wooden frame, which can be simply made using four timber laths of 18" by 2 ¾" each. These can be joined at the corners in a number of ways. *Fig. 8.12* shows one of these ways.

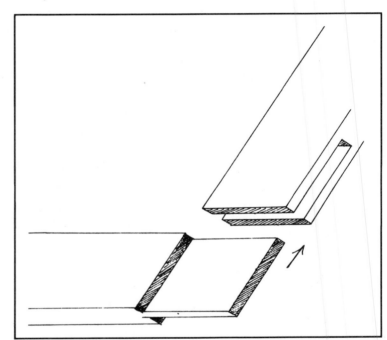

Fig. 8.12

Making a wooden frame

Organdie or screen-print mesh (or any close-meshed material) is then stretched tightly over the frame on one side. The mesh should be moistened first, so that it can be stretched to its tightest. Use a stapling gun or thumb tacks to fastening the fabric to the sides of the frame.

Screen Printing Dyes

Some of the screen printing dyes available come ready mixed, for instant use, thus saving much valuable time. For fabric printing, the type chosen should be oil-based. When the print has been made on the fabric, the fabric should be ironed — this will prevent the dye from fading or running when washed.

The Squeegee

This is an essential tool for the screen printing process. It consists of a wooden block with a thin strip of rubber embedded in one side — *Fig. 8.13.*

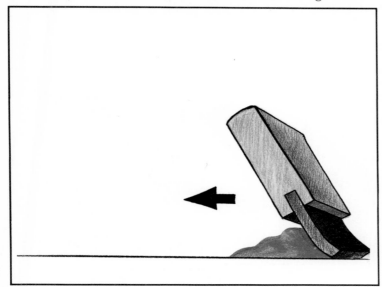

Fig. 8.13

Printing dye is forced through the screen by the squeegee, in one firm downward stroke. This stroke should be worked from top to bottom of the screen, with the ink load ahead of the squeegee rubber.

Screen Printing Stencils

In the fabric printing industry, sophisticated photographic stencils are used but tracing paper will suffice for student work. These stencils can be cut, as in the earlier exercises, with a craft knife — *Fig. 8.14* — or with a suitable cutting blade.

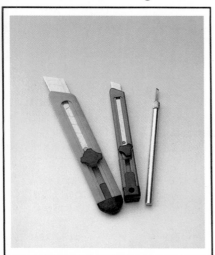

Fig. 8.14

Selection of craft knives suitable for cutting stencils

Making a Screen Print

As with other printing methods, screen printing designs are best kept simple. Make a few preliminary sketches until you feel the design is suitable for cutting.

In order to eliminate any leakage problems during printing, it is imperative that the stencil paper covers the entire screen surface area. Once you have made the stencil, assemble the cut-outs on a clean sheet of newsprint, and place the screen on top. Prime the top end of the screen with printing dye and make one downward stroke with the squeegee, drawing the dye before the rubber edge.

Fig. 8.15   The master design from which all stencils and tracings will be made

Fig. 8.16   Keylining

Fig. 8.17   Completing the design

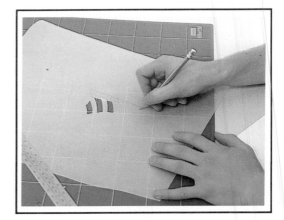

Fig. 8.18   Cutting the stencils on a cutting board

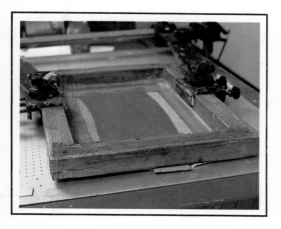

Fig. 8.19   On the screen. Note cardboard wedge — this ensures that the screen will lift from the print after the downward stroke of the squeegee.

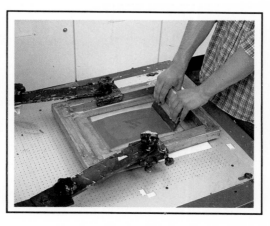

Fig. 8.20   Using the squeegee

Fig. 8.21   First prints

Fig. 8.22   Building the design

97

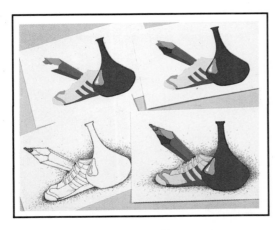

Fig. 8.23   Prints & overprints

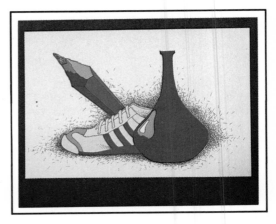

Fig. 8.24   The final image (cross hatch & black
outline produced by Tusche method)

Lithographic Tusche

In addition to cut-outs made with tracing paper, stencils can be made using the Tusche method. This technique requires the use of stencil medium (or masking fluid) and lith-ink. Ideally the screen for Tusche work should be fine meshed — circa 90 strands per cm².

Stencil medium is a water based compound, while lith-ink is oil based. This Tusche stencil making technique relies on the fact that water and oil do not mix.

The Tusche method of stencil making is as follows:

Using a steel pen charged with lith-ink, the design to be printed onto the screen is drawn. When the drawing is completed and is dry, a squeegee is used to spread the water based stencil medium over the entire screen. The stencil medium is 'repelled' (as it were) wherever the oily lith-ink lines occur.

When the stencil medium has dried, the lith-ink can be removed with an oil based thinner such as turpentine. (The stencil medium remains intact as it is unaffected by turpentine). What remains, therefore, is a permeable drawing outline, suitable for screen printing.

The finished stencil should be examined, in front of a bright light, for pin holes. If any are found, they can be masked by painting stencil medium directly onto the screen, using a small brush.

The Tusche method is ideal for detailed line drawing, as seen in *Fig. 8.16*. Here, a black line drawing and hatching is superimposed over the colour print.

A stencil can also be made by drawing directly onto the screen, using a brush charged with stencil medium.

9 Lettering

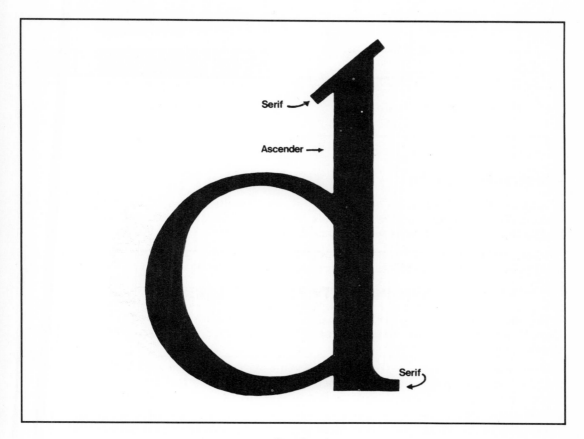

Serif

Ascender

Serif

Fig. 9.1

As an introduction to this interesting area of art, look at some posters, book covers, record sleeves, greeting cards, etc. and study the lettering. Notice the shape of the letters, the spacing between each letter, the clarity of the work, the different sizes of words (important words larger than the rest), the finish and the neatness of the lettering. Having done this, we can turn our attention to the technical aspects of the art of lettering.

Optical Illusion

An understanding of the effects of optical illusion is of paramount importance in all areas of visual design. This is particularly relevant when we consider alphabet design or the art of lettering. These illusions affect the visual impact of shape, and therefore should not be overlooked, as shape is the essence of lettering.

In *Fig. 9.2*, you will notice a series of *guidelines*. These lines are used to maintain a consistency in letter height. The normal ratio is ⅓:⅔; the lower case lettering occupying ⅔ of the space, while the remaining ⅓ is the additional writing area for upper case (capital) lettering.

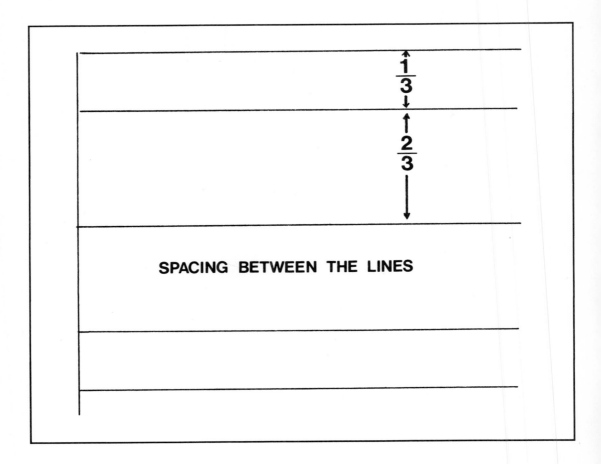

Fig. 9.2   Guidelines

Round Topped and Round Bottomed Letters

Letters which are curved or rounded, on top or bottom, must extend above or below the guideline; if they do not, they will appear to be smaller than their flat-topped/bottomed neighbours — *Fig. 9.3.*

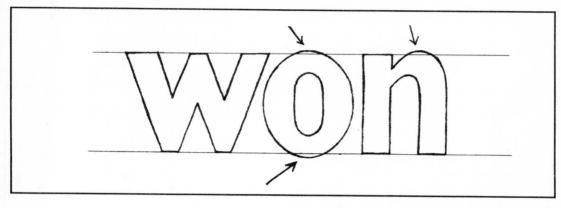

Fig. 9.3

Pointed Letters

Letters such as V, A, W, which have sharp points, must have these points extended above and/or below the guideline also. Otherwise they will appear to be either hanging from, or sitting on, the line — *Fig. 9.4.*

Fig. 9.4

101

The Division of a Square or Rectangle

In *Fig. 9.5*, we see a square divided in half by a horizontal line. The lower division looks smaller than the upper, despite the accuracy of measurement. To counteract this illusion, one has to draw the dividing line a little higher up in the square; the square then looks properly divided — *Fig. 9.6*.

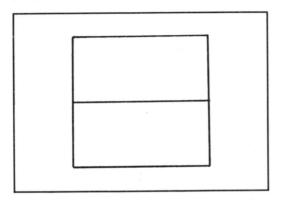
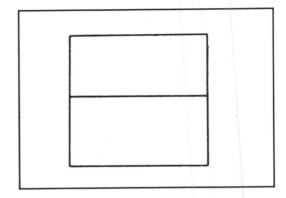

| Fig. 9.5 | Fig. 9.6 |

The division of the square is of great consequence when dealing with the placement of, say, the centre line of a capital E; ideally this line should not divide the letter into two equal halves.

The Perfect Square

One thing to remember about a square which is geometrically perfect, is that it appears to be a little wide to the eye — *Fig. 9.7*. To offset this illusion, its height should be slightly increased — *Fig. 9.8*.

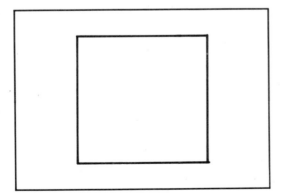
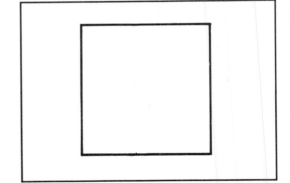

| Fig. 9.7 | Fig. 9.8 |

The Perfect Circle

Letters such as O, Q, C, should never be perfectly circular in shape. These letters look more pleasing when their height is narrower than their width, as in *Fig. 9.9.*

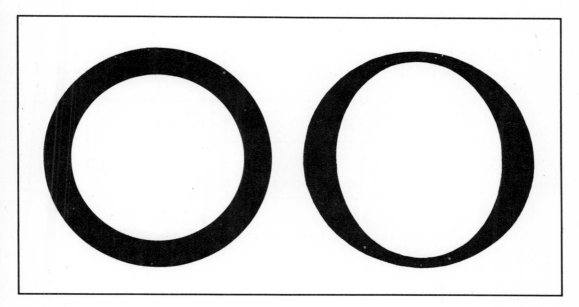

Fig. 9.9

The Spacing of Letters

Alphabets are designed primarily to form words for communication, as in newspapers, posters, advertments, etc. The ease with which we read these words depends largely on the Alphabet design itself and, very importantly, on the spacing of the letters.

As you well know, no two letters in the alphabet are the same shape; it is for this reason that the spacing between letters must vary.

Fig. 9.10 shows a selection of words, which together demonstrate the importance of correct letter spacing.

AVE	VAN	POOR	INO	All
AVE	VAN	PO OR	INO	All

Fig. 9.10

General Rules for Spacing Letters

Letters with parallel verticals, as in *Fig. 9.11*, need more space between them and following letters than do other letters.

Million	**Million**

Fig. 9.11

Rounded or curved sided letters can be spaced much closer, *Fig. 9.12*.

POOR	**PO OR**

Fig. 9.12

Letters such as **V W** and **A** often 'overlap' their neighbouring letter(s), *Fig. 9.13*. This mainly occurs in upper case (capitals).

AV	WA	V A

Fig. 9.13

Fig. 9.14 shows how **V** (similarly **W**) and **A** may be spaced when next to vertical letters.

All	Vince

Fig. 9.14

Fig. 9.15 shows how they may be spaced next to curved letters.

VOGUE	AS

Fig. 9.15

Alphabet and Typeface Designs

Despite the fact that there are only 26 letters in our alphabet, it is generally accepted that, artistically, typeface or alphabet design is a very difficult task. In trying to achieve balance and beauty, the typeface designer is confronted with problems such as the relationship of capitals to lower case letters and, above all else, with the issue of legibility. The design has to read clearly and yet be attractive to the eye.

Words are read by 'group impressions', i.e. not letter by letter. If, however, so much as one letter is poorly designed, ease of reading will be disrupted, and the typeface design may justly be regarded as unsuccessful.

All too often we see posters on notice boards which are barely legible; such work reflects poor knowledge of lettering or layout. *Fig. 9.16* shows some badly designed lettering.

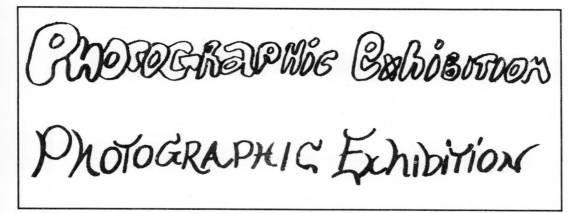

Fig. 9.16

Fig. 9.17 shows the same words using a well designed typeface.

Photographic Exhibition

Fig. 9.17

From these examples, it is obvious that one should not dabble with the design of letters. On the whole, letter design is best left to the experts.

A B C D E F G H
I J K L M N O P
Q R S T U V
W X Y Z

a b c d e f g h i j k
l m n o p q r s t u v
w x y z

Fig. 9.18 (top) Helvetica Capitals & Fig. 9.19 (btm) Helvetica lower case

A B C D E F G

H I J K L M

N O P Q R S T

U V W X Y Z

Fig. 9.20   Clarendon Bold Capitals

Note: When studying letters such as A H K U Y W Z X V N M, note carefully where the thick and thin lines are placed (applicable only to designs incorporating such strokes).

abcdefg
hijklm
nopqrst
uvwxyz

Fig. 9.21   Clarendon Bold lower case

Figs. 9.18 - 9.21 show two popular typeface designs which are regularly used in advertising, where clarity really matters. It is advisable that at least one of these should be learned and studied carefully. Pay particular attention to proportions, which may be examined by using a divider. You will see very quickly that letters vary in height and width, for instance, the letter W compared to the letter I.

Lettering can also be suggestive of an idea or a mood — e.g.

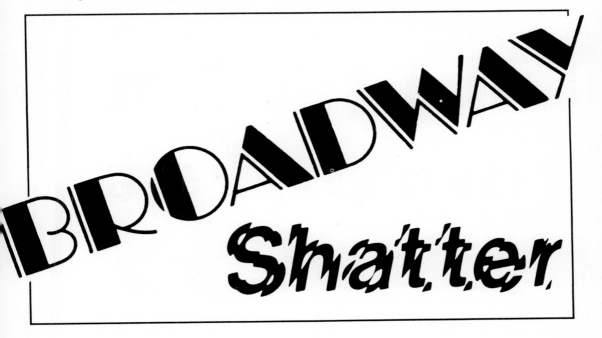

Fig. 9.22

Painting Letters

Once the letter shapes have been studied, we can turn our attention to drawing them lightly with pencil and painting in the shapes. Choose a long word and sketch the letters in capitals and then in lower case. When this is done, paint in the shapes.

Fig. 9.23 shows you how to hold a pencil and brush when painting in letter shapes.

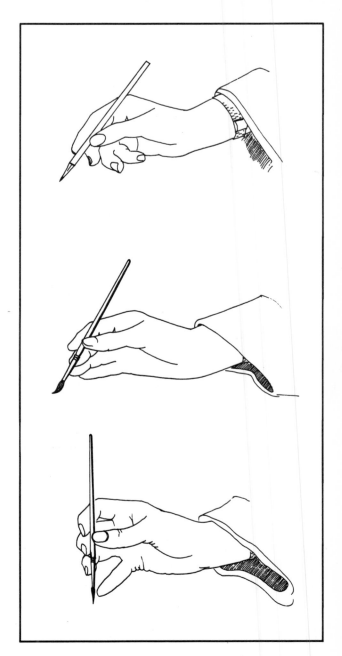

(a) How to hold a pencil;

(b) Brush position for normal use;

(c) Brush position for long strokes.

Fig. 9.23

How to paint a neat edge, a useful technique when working with large lettering. Notice that the hairs of the brush are pressed flat during the stroke.

Fig. 9.24

Assignments

1. Using the capitals and lower case of Helvetica or Clarendon, form the following words (letters should be at least 4-5 cms in height):

   TASTE ILLUSION STILL MOORE WASTE.

2. Copy five capital letters of your choice, excluding I, from the selection of type-face designs in this chapter.

3. To experiment with the spacing of letters, make paper cut-outs of letters which you have copied. Juggle these letters about, not to form new words, but to examine spacing.

4. Take cuttings of a variety of typeface designs from magazines, suggesting ideas such as Shock; Crash; High-Class Fashion; Speed.

5. Write out the words in Q.1 using one of the other alphabet designs in this chapter.

6. Centre the following words on a page using a vertical centring line:

   DESIGNER CITY DENTIST BOOT SHOOT.

   First count the number of letters so as to find the middle letter (make allowances for different letter widths) and then work outward from the vertical centring line.

Calligraphy

Calligraphy pen with selection of nibs and some examples of the beautiful handwriting possible using this implement.

Fig. 9.25

Calligraphy is the art of handwriting, or hand-lettering, using nibs. Fountain pens for this art form are relatively inexpensive and usually come with a wide selection of nibs. Ink-well pens may also be used but are time-consuming and tend to blob easily. Should you decide to use an ink-well pen, the purchase of a reservoir attachment for the nib is advisable.

The first thing you will notice about your calligraphy pen is the variety of nib widths; the different sizes enable you to make thick and thin strokes. A downward stroke of the nib produces a wide line, whilst a diagonal one produces a narrow line. This variation in line width is a key aspect of the beauty of calligraphy.

Many calligraphers have a preference for black ink, as it shows up the variation of line thickness very clearly against a white background. Black ink is also the traditional writing medium. Inks other than black are less definite and uneveness of ink flow is easily detected, resulting in "patchy" lettering.

Fig. 9.26
*The correct angle at which to hold
a calligraphy pen.*

Fig. 9.27 shows the practice strokes necessary for accurate control of the calligraphy pen.

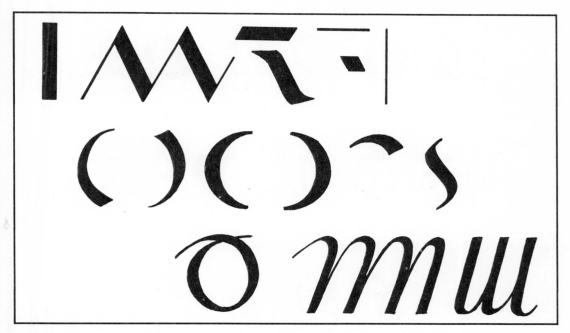

Fig. 9.27

Figs. 9.28-31 display two alphabet designs which are well suited to calligraphy work:
Old English & Zapf Chancery.

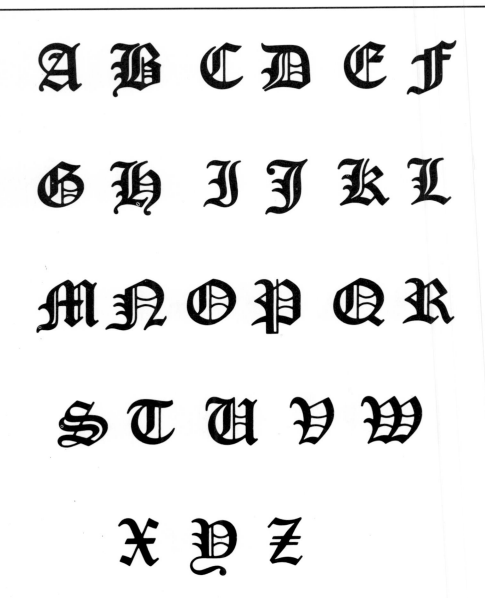

Fig. 9.28   Old English Capitals

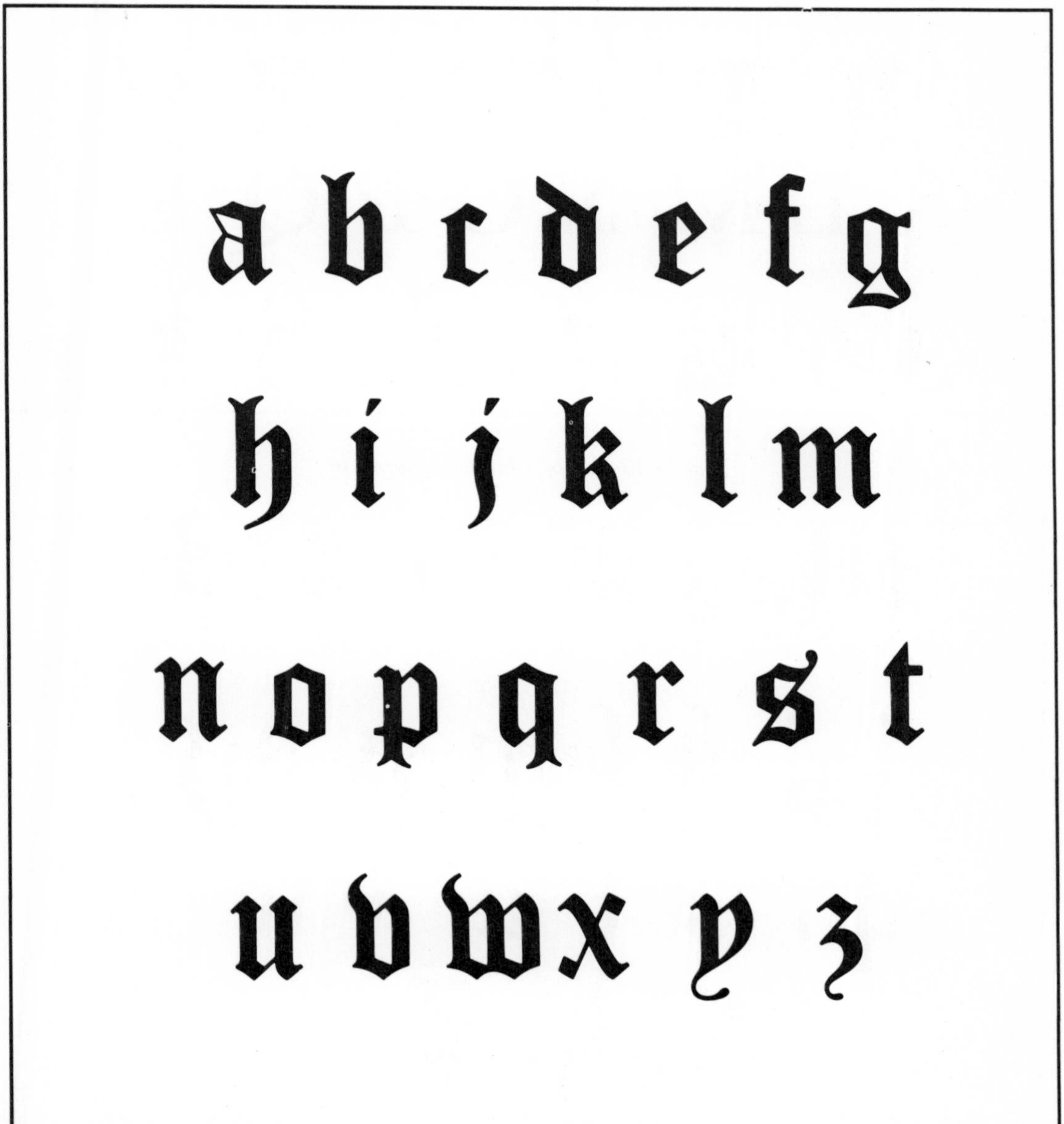

a b c d e f g

h i j k l m

n o p q r s t

u v w x y z

Fig. 9.29   Old English lower case

ABCDEFGHIJ
KLMNOPQR
STUVWXYZ

Fig. 9.30   *Zapf Chancery Capitals*

a b c d e f g h
i j k l m n o p
q r s t u v w
x y z

Fig. 9.31   *Zapf Chancery lower case*

Margins

When drawing margins, the space below the boundary at the bottom of the page should always be larger than the space at the top of the page. The side margins should be of equal size; their width will depend on the amount of words per line and on the width of the nib which is being used.

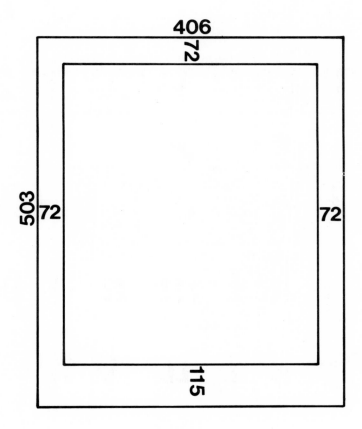

Fig. 9.32

With the page properly ruled and laid out, mark in lightly, in pencil, the wording of the first line. This practice is worthwhile because it lets you know how many letters and words will fit into a line. Mis-spelling can also be easily corrected at this stage, using an eraser.

Page Layout

As earlier noted, guidelines for capital and lower case letters are an essential aid to lettering. Their ratio is usually ⅔ for lower case and an additional ⅓ for capitals. (Note that metric measurement is generally more efficient than imperial.) If a wide nib is chosen, then the guideline should be wide enough to accomodate the thickness of the strokes — otherwise lettering will be restricted and blobs are likely to occur.

The space between the lines should be slightly less than the height of a lower case letter *(see back, Fig. 9.2).*

If you intend doing many lines of lettering, a useful tip is to make an accurate measurement of the guidelines, and of the space between lines, on a small piece of paper and use this repeatedly as a reference down along the page margin.

Assignments

1. Write out the following poem:

The Lady of Shallot

On either side the river lie
Long fields of barley and of rye
That clothe the wold and meet the sky;
And thro' the field the road runs by
To many-towered Camelot;
And up and down the people go;
Gazing where the lilies grow;
Round an island there below
The island of Shallot.

Alfred Tennyson

2. Write out a stanza from any other poem of your choice.

10 Design

Design is an area of art which relies on the artist's ability to couple artistic beauty with suitability of purpose. As discussed in *Chapter 9*, there is little or no point in designing a fanciful typeface, if legibility suffers as a result. Similarly, a potter will not design a vessel which does not perform the function for which it is intended. A good designer must be fully aware of the limitations of the medium with which he/she is working; if not, there will be many disasters along the way!

In this chapter, we will be dealing with marketing/advertising design, taking Poster and Record Sleeve design as topics for study. The principles outlined, however, can also be applied to Book Cover design, Invitation Cards, Wrapping Paper, etc.

Posters

The primary function of a poster is to convey information quickly and effectively. Well executed lettering, which is properly spaced and laid out correctly, goes a long way in serving this purpose.

Posters fall into two basic categories:

1. Those which rely mainly on the written word.
2. Those which incorporate a strong visual stimulus, e.g. clever use of colour, motif, or something which generally attracts the eye.

Category 1

In this type of poster, the most important wording will receive priority of letter size. Other headings will be smaller, depending on their importance. The aim is to achieve maximum impact. It is important on largely verbal posters to avoid cluttering, as this will only cause confusion and the poster will lose its effectiveness.

Category 2

This type of poster relies mainly on visual stimulus. In designing such posters, students are often tempted to clutter the poster with pictorial compositions and with poorly formed lettering. Simple ideas work best. Impact is essential.

Fig. 10.1   Category 1 type poster (hand-painted)
by Pat Burns

The Melvyn Tuttle Trio

Fig. 10.2

Category 2 type poster
by Anne Siggins, graphic designer
(above)

Fig. 10.3   Preparatory sketches

Poster Design

As with lino cuts and screen print designs, many preliminary sketches should be made to refine the original idea — *Fig. 10.3*. Simplify each sketch until a strong pattern emerges. The design should also be suited to the page format, so keep this in mind during the rough sketches. How are you going to incorporate the lettering? Is the design good enough to attract attention? These are considerations which you should be keenly aware of at the preparatory stages.

To experiment with alternative placements of the title over the design, fasten a sheet of tracing paper onto the page; rule in the guidelines and draw the letters. When this is completed, you can lift the tracing paper and move the title about, to examine various placing possibilities. Once you have decided on a position, trace the title onto the page.

Layout

Rule the upper and lower margins of the page; the space above the boundary at the top of the page should be smaller than that at the bottom, as discussed in *Calligraphy*. Now rule the side margins. These should be equal in size, and preferably not too close to the edge of the page. Finally, rule a vertical centering line from top to bottom — *Fig. 10.4*.

The vertical line is for the centering of the wording. Count the number of letters in each word, to establish the mid-point. Jot this data down on paper and keep it aside for later use. Rule in the guidelines with a T-Square or a Set Square, based on the proportions of the rough sketches. Pay particular attention to the interlinear (between lines) spacing. Select a typeface from *Chapter 9* and rough in the letters with a pencil, working out from the centre line, *Fig. 10.4*.

The mid-point of a word may not be the middle letter, since letters vary in width. Make allowances for such letters as capital I, W and O; lower case i; etc.

When you have finished the rough lettering and are happy with the centring and lay-out, you can define the letter shapes more accurately.

Colour

If you are working on a white background it is better to employ at most two colours. Dark reds and blues are quite effective because of their contrast with white. Alternatively you can paint all the letters black, which will also provide good contrast.

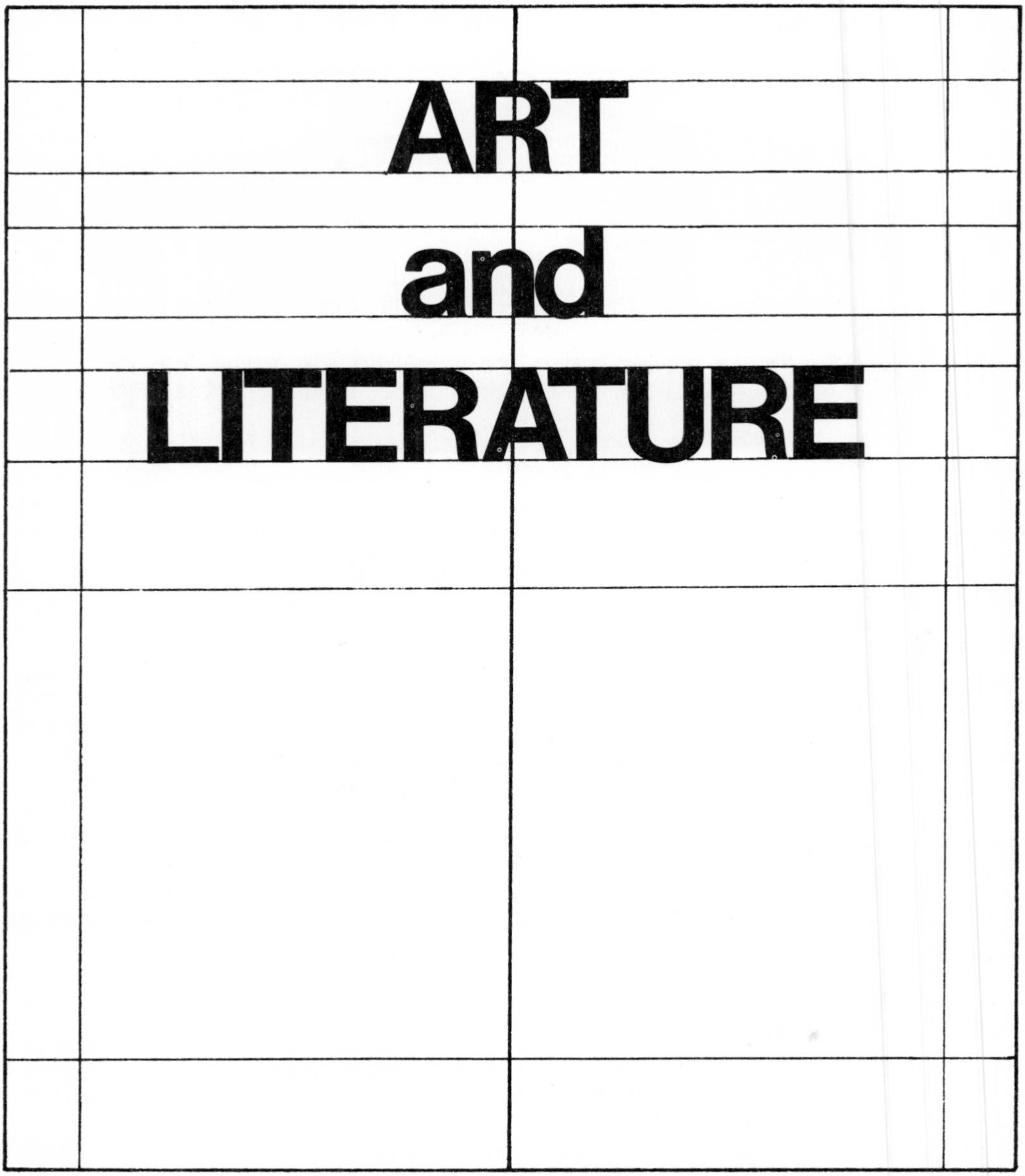

ART
and
LITERATURE

Fig. 10.4   Page Layout

Record Sleeve Design

Fig. 10.5   Record Sleeve designs

Note the striking effect of simple visuals and good use of typeface against a black backround

The first thing to consider when designing a Record Sleeve is the theme. What image do the musicians wish to convey? Take the following title as an example:

* Disco Nite Out *

Jot down all the ideas that this title brings to mind:

Disco — Dance, Neon Lights, Glitter, Glamour, Mirrors, Disc Jockeys, Movement, People, Records, Couples, City or town, Cocktail bars, Beat, Pulse, Energy, Types of clothing ...

Nite Out — Spelling suggests an American flavour, Dark, Extravaganza, City Skyline, Stars, Moon, Traffic ...

These are some of the obvious associations; perhaps you can think of more unusual ones. Develop some ideas under one or more of these headings, and make a few sketches, just as you did for the poster designs. Make a special allowance for the title of the record, and work on a square format (for albums 12" by 12" and singles 7" by 7").

As a general rule, record sleeves, as opposed to posters, rely on pictorial images, with lettering less dominant. This is not, however, to dismiss the importance of the title.

Fig. 10.6   Record Sleeves where pictorial image is dominant

Note particularly the middle sleeve, which is a striking monochrome design

Design on Packaging

Select some commodity that you buy regularly, e.g. shampoo, soap, soup, tin of beans, etc. and write down what you think makes this commodity sell so well:

Images — on the box/tin/package/etc.?
Lettering — the image it helps to create?
Slogan — catchy?
Competition — free holiday, etc.?
Free Offer — two for the price of one, etc.?

Fig. 10.8   Supermarket shopping, where packaging can greatly influence choice

Now select a product which *you* feel is poorly presented and re-design the packaging, taking into consideration all the design elements with which you are now familiar (colour, shape, texture, images, etc.). Finally, make the new packaging out of cardboard and/or other available materials, as per your design.